BUSINESS ETIQUETTE IN BRIEF

THE COMPETITIVE EDGE FOR TODAY'S PROFESSIONAL

Ann Marie Sabath

BOB ADAMS, INC.
PUBLISHERS
Holbrook, Massachusetts

Published by Bob Adams, Inc.
260 Center Street, Holbrook, MA 02343

ISBN: 1-55850-254-8

Printed in Canada

J   I

This publication is designed to provide accurate and authoritative information with regard to the subject matter covered. It is sold with the understanding that the publisher is not engaged in rendering legal, accounting, or other professional advice. If legal advice or other expert assistance is required, the services of a competent professional person should be sought.
— From a *Declaration of Principles* jointly adopted by a Committee of the American Bar Association and a Committee of Publishers and Associations

This book is available at quantity discounts for bulk purchases.
For information, call 1-800-872-5627 (in Massachusetts, 781-767-8100).

Visit our exciting small business Web site at businesstown.com

Acknowledgments

My acknowledgments go . . .

To my parents, Mary and Camille Sabath, who gave me life.

To my children, Scott and Amber, who ate many microwave dinners while I was busily documenting the proper way to dine.

To Budahan, my loyal 13-year-old schnauzer, who forfeited walks only to patiently lie at my feet while I pounded away on the computer.

To my sister, Patty, who was always there when I needed to brainstorm.

To my many corporate clients and column readers, whose questions were an invaluable asset to the creation of this book.

To Maxine Elliott-Nason, who edited my business etiquette columns from day one.

To my wonderful At Ease Inc. staff, who assisted in answering the Etiquette Hotline.

To Julie Lawlor, who believed in business etiquette enough to do a story in *USA Today*.

To Bob Adams, of Bob Adams, Inc., who approached me to write this book.

To Bob Adams' grandmother, who according to Bob, "stressed the importance of etiquette to me so much that I saw a need for a book on this topic."

To my dear friend and colleague, Rose Huber, who breathed life into this book.

To my Managing Editor, Brandon Toropov, who was either always available to accept my telephone calls, or returned my calls promptly—either because he is polite by nature or for fear of committing a telephone courtesy "faux pas."

To Kate Layzer, who diplomatically extended her pinky and pencil to make the changes that took this manuscript from its rough to its polished form.

To that special man in my life . . .

And most significantly, to the Power above, who gave me the inspiration and stamina to sit still long enough to put my thoughts on paper.

— Ann Marie Sabath
January, 1993

Contents

Introduction

How many times have you heard it? *It's the little things that count.*

Trite as this axiom might sound, nowhere does it hold more truth and power than in the competitive world of business—where the little niceties and social amenities, those things I call the *half-percents*, can mean the difference between simply existing and gaining the edge so necessary for success in today's fiercely competitive business environment.

As you read through this book, you'll learn dozens of *half-percents* designed to help set you apart as a polished and practiced professional. For your convenience, I've included a key symbol ⊶ before each. These common-sense tips are the results of my own experience, of research, and of feedback at the hundreds of workshops and seminars I have conducted since establishing At Ease Inc. in 1987.

Before founding my company, which specializes in business etiquette and protocol, I used to think the term *etiquette* described frivolous gestures like extending your pinky when lifting a glass of white wine or keeping your elbows off the table while dining.

Was I ever wrong!

It wasn't long before I learned that business etiquette has a very simple and practical definition—*Knowing what to do and when.*

In many cases, perhaps the majority, you probably already know what to do and when. This book has been developed to reinforce your confidence. It is also intended to help you safely past those numerous *moments of hesitation* you may experience when interacting with others—ear to ear, face to face, and through correspondence. We all experience these brief, uncomfortable periods when we're not quite sure how to get a conversation started, who to introduce to whom, etc. This book offers practical guidelines.

Dress is not the problem. These days, most business people know and adhere to the appropriate definitions of professional attire. However, many companies have reached the point where they're saying to themselves, "Well, we can dress them up. But can we take them out?" This is why business etiquette seminars and workshops have met with overwhelming enthusiasm and success these last few years. It's also the reason for this book.

With its no-nonsense, common-sense approach, *Business Etiquette in Brief* has been designed not for the blue-blooded (who have been schooled in the social graces from childhood) but for ordinary red-blooded people like you and me, who make up the majority of today's vibrant and vital work force. The information presented is intended as a practical guide for those moving through the various phases of evolving professional success.

In some instances the information in this book is presented as a series of "rules." These admonitions should seldom, if ever, be broken. In other cases the suggestions and tips are merely guidelines to apply to your particular business culture—using your common sense. Traditionally, for instance, advertising agencies and newspaper offices display a more relaxed dress code and business environment than, say, a Fortune 500 corporation. You're more likely to see a newspaper editor sporting loafers and a sport coat than wing-tips and a two-piece suit.

Look around you before setting on a style of dress for yourself. As you read about such things as half-percents and moments of hesitation, you may ask yourself, *Who in the world came up with these rules?* Maybe it was your mother or grandmother. Perhaps even your great-grandmother. Who knows, it may very well have been one of your male ancestors. The point is, the unwritten rules of business etiquette were most likely created by people like you and me—and for quite practical reasons. They were simply ways to extend human courtesies to one another.

The world has changed since those days. It's become high-tech and complicated. Yet these basic courtesies have never gone out of style. Quite the contrary: In today's business environment they become even more crucial to gaining a competitive edge. Why? Just consider the following.

- ◆ *Automation has become an integral part of our lives.* Like it or not, innovations like voice mail, facsimile machines, and electronic mail are here to stay. And the more high-tech our world becomes, the more important effective inter personal communication will be.

◆ *Men and women have become colleagues.* Each year women continue to be promoted to management positions—but not without kinks. Social rules from yesteryear are suddenly called into question. Men today are asking questions like,

"Is it appropriate for me to initiate a handshake before a woman extends her hand?"

"If the woman sitting next to me leaves the table for a fleeting moment, should I stand?"

"When introducing my female manager to a male customer, whose name should I say first during the introduction?"

Likewise, women are asking,

"When a man approaches me, should I stand?"

"When taking a male client to lunch, how can I tactfully let the server know that I will be picking up the check?"

"What can I do when a man shakes my fingers rather than my hand?"

These questions and many others will be covered in the chapters that follow.

◆ *Many of today's young business people are part of the McManners Drivethru Generation.* Despite the fact that numerous trips to the fast food lane may not have exposed this generation to some of the table manners basic to those reared in less frenzied times, today's young professionals are still expected to possess a certain degree of finesse once they enter the business world. As students make the transition from college to the work force, it is crucial for them to recognize that, no matter what company they will be representing, a corporate culture awaits them. If they are astute, these young professionals soon realize that employers expect new hires both to recognize and to adapt quickly to their organization's culture.

Unfortunately, companies are finding that many of their new hires don't have a clue about the existing culture. They can no longer assume that, just because the new employee is armed with one or more academic de-

grees and impressive professional credentials, basics like polished manners are included in the deal. Why not? In many cases, parents of these young women and men never taught them that social rules are a given. Perhaps they weren't at home long enough to tell their young-sters things like,
   "Sit up straight!"
   "Chew with your mouth closed!"
   "Don't hold your fork as though it were a shovel!"
   If you grew up in the absence of such guidelines, think of this book as continuing education.

◆ *We live in a global marketplace.* Whether you find yourself entertaining international clients in your own backyard or conducting business abroad, a working knowledge of cross-cultural communication is paramount for building healthy and productive professional relationships. We need to be aware that verbal or non-verbal gestures that we view as perfectly acceptable in the United States may be a major faux pas in other parts of the world. Since the topic of communicating with international visitors is an extensive one, it's been given only a cursory treatment in this book. To do the subject justice requires a book it-self. For that reason, I've included a list of excellent books on the subject in the list of recommended read-ings.

Does all this sound intimidating? It shouldn't. In fact, you probably already possess the instincts needed to master those little details that count for so much in business. Success today still means three things: hard work, honesty, and good manners. By conscientiously giving your best and by extending to your associ-ates the same consideration you would like them to show you—by employing the crucial half-percents you'll read about in this book—you will already boast a competitive edge.

Take hard work. If you try to get by with doing the mini-mum, if you live for breaks, if you make and accept personal phone calls on a regular basis during working hours . . . if you show that you do not value your position by not giving it your all, then you are simply not putting your best self forward.

As for honesty, how many times have you told an internal associate (colleague, manager, employee) or an external one (customer, client) that you would call him or her back by a certain time—say 3 p.m. on Thursday? How many times have you not been able to reach the person who has the information you need to enable you to return the call by the time you promised?

By extending the courtesy of placing your call by Thursday at 3 p.m. anyway and explaining to the person that you are still waiting for a call-back from someone who has the needed information, there is a good chance that you will be perceived as honest and as a person who does, indeed, follow through.

If, however, you do not get back to the person by the designated time, hoping that he or she assumes that your lack of follow-up indicates you do not have the required information, you may or may not be perceived as dishonest; but you probably *will* run the risk of souring a business relationship.

Little things, you may say. And you're right.

But they're little things that pay off in a big way. They're the half-percents that can truly give you the competitive edge.

1.

How to Make a Positive and Powerful First Impression

As you've doubtless been told time and time again, it takes only ten or fifteen seconds to make a first impression—and the rest of your life to undo it, if it's a negative one. With practice, you can learn to present yourself as a polished professional every time you meet someone. Here are some guidelines to get you off on the right foot.

Four rules for making a good impression
Since body language and words both play a major role in how you are perceived by others, let's look at four rules that address the first impressions we present to others. Remember, the half-percents you're learning are marked by the ⊶ .

⊶ **1. Make your first 10 words count.** The most effective way to open any interaction is to send a "thanks" message.
"Thank you for taking the time to meet with me this morning, Mr. Smith."
"It's a pleasure to finally meet you in person, Miss Wright."
These are excellent thanks messages for first-time meetings. You can also use this rule effectively with people you already know. For example,
"Thanks for your interest in getting together, Barbara."
"Dennis, thank you for suggesting we meet."
⊶ When possible, include the person's name in the first ten or twelve words of conversation.
"It's great seeing you again, Charlie."
Admit it. Most of us tune in when we hear our names. We all

enjoy personal recognition, no matter how modest. So start on a positive note and recognize the person you're speaking to.

━० **2. Tune into others.** Make eye contact. Wear a smile. Your expression can convey energy and motivation or gloom and depression. Consider . . . Do you prefer to meet with someone who looks as if she's had a bad night? Or with someone with a smile on her face and a twinkle in her eye? Your expressions demonstrate the confidence you have in yourself. Smile. Be vibrant. Be confident. And people will respond positively. Try it. It works.

━० **3. Walk with a purpose.** Whether you're walking into your office building or are on your way to meet clients, put some bounce into your step. Move with vigor and vitality.

Most of us enjoy being around high-energy people. Try walking at the end of a long day with the same early morning zest you enjoy at the beginning of a day. Others will notice that extra bounce and energy.

━० **4. Be impeccably groomed.** The succeeding chapters will deal with specific tips on professional dress for men and women, but positive first impressions dictate a few basic considerations.

━० Keep your hair neat and in a fashion that flatters the shape of your face.

━० Wear jewelry appropriate to the event and situation. The quality of jewelry and accessory items worn is often perceived as a reflection of the kind of person you are.

━० Men, use the one-finger test when buying shirts. To make sure a shirt fits properly, place your index finger between the collar and your neck. If there's enough room to slip your finger comfortably into the space, you are not only assured of an excellent fit, you will also feel less compelled to unbutton the top button.

━० Calling all men and women: Start off on the right foot. Give the same attention to the grooming of your shoes that you do to your hair and clothing. Shoes should be so well maintained that they look like new.

━० Women should also be aware of the poor impression made by hosiery with runners. Always keep an extra pair of stockings at work—just in case.

━० And, men . . . please know that most women love to

see a little leg, but *not* when you're wearing trousers. Wear socks that cover your calves when seated.

Seven easy ways to sabotage a first impression
Try as we might to make that all-important first impression a positive one, it's easy to fall into one of the following very common manners traps.

1. Sloppy language. Most of us are products of our environment. In many instances the words we use and the way in which we use them are based on what we heard our parents say. I was thirty years old before anyone told me that *anyways* is not a word. I wish someone had told me sooner. Was I embarrassed? Certainly! Was I grateful to the person who discreetly corrected me? You bet!

Are you using terms that are not correct? If you're not sure and want to find out, I highly recommend you invest in *Word Watcher's Handbook* by St. Martin's Press. Author Phyllis Martin provides a handy dictionary of some of the most abused and misused words making their way into business and social conversations today.

➝ Use a vocabulary appropriate to the situation.

2. Using lazy words. No matter how well you dress and how many initials you have after your name, using sloppy words will lessen your credibility with others. Some examples are *yeah* rather than *yes*, *you guys* rather than *you*, and *okey dokey* rather than *all right*.

➝ Choose your words carefully.

3. Giggling. While laughter can be the best medicine for many ills, giggling can be downright annoying. Some people giggle to fill silent or awkward moments. They should simply pause instead. Giggling is a distracting and unprofessional habit.

➝ Don't giggle.

4. Inappropriate touching. The only legitimate form of touch in business is the handshake. Unless you've established a rapport with someone, a pat, nudge, or touch on the arm can be perceived as too friendly.

➝ Keep your hands where they belong.

5. Hiding your hands. Believe it or not, etiquette research has shown that hands above board are more appealing than hands hidden away in pockets. When your hands are not showing, it often sends a signal to someone that you are not telling all or that you're holding something back. So if you're one of those people who can't talk without using your hands, consider yourself fortunate. Others might wish to cultivate that habit. If you don't overdo it, the extra action helps you come off as an energized, enthusiastic person. At any rate, if you're not prone to gesturing, at least keep your hands where they can be seen.

6. Gumchewing. Let there be no doubt about it. Chewing gum does not belong in the work place. No exceptions. If you enjoy chewing gum, indulge yourself on your personal time. During the work day you may very well be perceived as unprofessional.

    ➤—0 Don't chew gum in the work place.

7. Throat clearing. The habit of clearing your throat several times during a conversation can be very distracting. Having the occasional urge to clear your throat is one thing. But if it becomes an annoying habit, try swallowing instead. When you swallow, it will seem to others to be merely a pause. Instead of being a distraction, this mini-moment of silence can even work to gain the attention of the person with whom you're speaking.

    ➤—0 When the urge to clear your throat becomes a habit, try swallowing instead.

Commonly Asked Questions About First Impressions

Q. In my opinion, the phrase, "What can I do for you?" is very condescending. How does it rate with you?

A. You have my vote. Phrases such as "How can I help you?" or "How may I be of assistance to you?" have a much better ring.

Q. Do you have any tips for projecting confidence? I've just changed jobs and would like to start out on the right foot.

A. Here are a few suggestions.

    ➤—0 Always be a few minutes early for appointments. It will demonstrate that you're in control of your time.

━0 Be organized. For instance, keep your business cards and pen in fixed locations so you won't have to search for them.

━0 Surround yourself with a team of confident staff members. When they project self-assurance, they will be a positive reflection of you.

2.

Professional Image Tips for Men

"I firmly believe that what gives others a sense of what and who you are is the way you are dressed. It is the first impression. I can't think of a man who, whether in business or at leisure, does not want to project authority."
— Bill Blass, *New York Magazine*

Adapting to the culture of your work place

It's a fact of life. We judge books by their covers and people by their clothes. Your image, therefore, is vital to landing a job and keeping it.

These days that image involves adapting to the culture of your particular work place. Some companies, for example, expect male employees to wear a suit at all times. Other organizations are comfortable with male associates wearing a sport coat and trousers. What's important is knowing what is considered appropriate in the company you represent.

The image you portray through your apparel is vital to how others perceive you. Whether you are a traditionalist or a fashion-forward trend setter, your business wardrobe should be geared to the culture of the company that employs you.

Suits

Most companies with rigid cultures encourage male employees to wear single-breasted, as opposed to double-breasted, suits. The reason is that the American (or single-breasted) jacket provides a more classic look, while the European (or double-breasted) jacket gives a more trendy or fashion-forward image.

No matter which of these styles a man chooses, certain buttons should be fastened when walking or standing. In the case of the American-cut jacket, the top of two buttons or the middle of three should be fastened. With a European cut, every button should be fastened.

Fabrics

➼ 100-percent wool blends (especially wool gabardine) are good choices for men's suits. When purchasing a suit, the scrunch test (to determine that the fabric is wrinkle-free) is a must. Gently squeeze the material between your hands. When you let go, does it wrinkle? If so, think twice before purchasing it. A suit should look as crisp at an afternoon meeting as it does when you first put it on in the morning.

Shirts

It goes without saying that long-sleeved shirts test best in business. White shirts portray the most formal look, especially when accompanied by stays, while light blue shirts give a more casual appearance. A button-down collar shirt (in one of many color choices) gives a less formal or preppy look to a suit jacket or sport coat.

Although many men do not wear undershirts, they should. The reasons are threefold. An undershirt:

◆ Keeps a dress shirt from feeling itchy against the skin.

◆ Preserves the shirt from perspiration.

◆ Gives added body to a dress shirt.

Ties

➼ When it comes to ties, width is what counts. Ties today should be between 2¾ and 3½ inches wide. I always suggest that the tip of the tie touch the top of a man's belt buckle.

Suspenders, or braces

➼ Americans have always called them "suspenders"; the British, "braces." Now the term "braces" is becoming more current in our country. By whatever name, when suspenders or braces are worn, the tie should reach the top of the waistband. If you choose suspenders for your wardrobe, be sure to wear those that button rather than clip on.

Belts and shoes

When selecting belts and shoes, think of black and cordovan as fashion-wise investments. While tassel loafers are acceptable with suits in some business cultures, wing-tips portray a more conservative look.

Accessories

The right accessory can enhance a man's wardrobe. Your image can take on added dimensions with details as simple as the pen you carry.

Pocket squares. This is strictly optional. Some men use this accessory to add a finishing touch to their suits. Others prefer to pass.

    ➼ If you enjoy wearing this accessory and you belong to a rigid corporate culture, play it safe and wear it for business gatherings after 5 p.m. If, however, you work in a more creative environment (fashion industry, advertising, etc.) your organization's culture may be open to pocket squares during business hours as well as after the work day has ended.

    ➼ In either case, be sure the pocket square you select complements your tie. You do not want the fabrics to match. Beware of retailers who sell matching ties and pocket scarves! This duo will definitely brand you as unfashionable.

Jewelry. Unless your male boss wears an earring, bracelet, or necklace with his business attire, my recommendation is that you keep this jewelry out of business life. A wedding band, class ring or other non-gaudy ring may be worn on the ring finger.

    The watch that blends best with business suits is one with a basic black leather or metal band. Plastic watchbands, which make you look as if you're ready to take off in the next marathon, should not be worn in business environments.

    ➼ **Pens.** The pen you carry should be perceived as an accessory. Believe it or not, it can say volumes about your confidence and business savvy (or lack of it). A high-quality writing instrument contributes to a polished image.

Dress-down days. The progressive nineties have brought a new wrinkle to office attire—dress-down days.

    Many companies, even some of the most traditional, are now

setting aside one day a week as a lighten-up kind of day where apparel is concerned. Notice of this contemporary trend and specific guidelines are generally issued.

Men, for instance, may be invited to dispense with ties, trade in their business suits for trousers and jacket—even wear jeans and a casual shirt with a collar.

Your particular business climate will dictate what is appropriate. When in doubt, ask. Or simply look around to see what your trusted colleagues are wearing.

Eight common fashion faux pas

Before you go out the door to work, double-check to make sure you're not committing one or more of the eight-most-commonly sighted fashion faux pas. To put things in a positive perspective, remember to observe the following half-percent image tips:

- Always wear a long-sleeved shirt with a suit.
- Make sure your shirt gives the appearance of having been professionally pressed.
- Be sure the tip of your tie touches the top of your belt buckle.
- Wear socks that reach mid-calf to avoid showing a flash of leg.
- When wearing an American-cut jacket (single-breasted), button up when standing or walking. If your jacket has two buttons, button the top one. If it has three, button the center one.
- When wearing a European-cut jacket (double-breasted), button all the buttons when standing or walking.
- Resole shoes with badly worn heels.
- Choose leather or metal watch bands.

Commonly Asked Questions About Image Tips for Men

Q. When is it appropriate for men to remove their jackets? I've frequently seen my boss remove his jacket before he sits down in a meeting with customers. Sometimes I question why he even wears one.

A. Business etiquette dictates that a jacket be removed only when the person who has arranged the meeting invites others to do so.

Q. When referring to attire, what does "business casual" mean?

A. This term has frequently been misinterpreted to mean "sloppy" by people who have been invited to company get-togethers or dinners following golf outings. As professionals, you have the responsibility to dress properly as well as comfortably.

For men, business casual can be defined as a crisp pair of slacks with a matching sports shirt and well-maintained footwear. Depending on the occasion, a sport coat may also be appropriate.

3.

Professional Image Tips for Women

"Costly thy habit as thy purse can buy,
But not express'd in fancy; rich, not gaudy,
For the apparel oft proclaims the man . . ."
— William Shakespeare, *Hamlet*

What tests best?
If Shakespeare were living in these much-changed times, he would certainly have addressed his caution statement to both sexes. The point, however, is well taken. Dressing for success can be tricky.

While you want your clothing to be a reflection of your personality, you know that to get ahead in the business world you should base your dress on what tests best.

You may have spent thousands of dollars and a lot of work and energy to earn a degree; and, no doubt, you have acquired great product knowledge. But your appearance remains one of the main factors that will encourage others to want to work with and for you.

When investing in business attire, select clothing that makes a positive statement. Though tailored dresses with shoulder pads (giving the illusion of more height) are quite acceptable today, the classic suit still portrays the most authority. Perhaps that's why it has remained the standard business uniform for me.

Women, look the part
Dress for the job you want, not for the job you have. Whoever came up

with this advice was very astute. Whether the dress code in the organization you represent is written or unwritten, you can bet there is one. If your company code is not documented as part of your organization's policies and procedures, simply look around. What is the company president wearing? What about your manager?

Many people are promoted because of their track records. Others seem to get there by default. In either case, it certainly didn't hurt them to look the part.

Suits

When building a professional wardrobe, you can't go wrong with high-quality suits in navy, grey, taupe, and black tones. These serve a definite purpose and are a must for every woman's business wardrobe. Brighter colors have a different function, adding fashion and flair. With a watchful eye on what's considered acceptable in your corporate environment, you'll be able to determine what colors and shades are and are not appropriate to your setting.

As for skirt lengths . . . Appropriate skirt lengths really depend on the industry you represent and, most importantly, on your company's culture. Generally speaking, skirts should be no shorter than slightly above the knee and fall no lower than just below mid-calf. Though mini-skirts might be "in," fashionwise, they have no place in a professional environment (unless you're working in retail or the like).

Fabrics

Just as important as the style and color of your suits are the fabrics you choose.

━━0 As I said in the chapter geared for men, when purchasing a suit, always apply the scrunch test to determine whether the fabric is wrinkle-free. If you skipped the chapter on men's attire, I'll repeat the instructions.

Gently squeeze the material between your hands. When you let go, is it wrinkled? If so, think twice before purchasing it. A suit should look as crisp for an afternoon meeting as it does when you put it on in the morning.

Fabrics that test well include 100-percent wool, wool blends, and silks. Some man-made fabrics that give the same appearance as these fabrics can also be wise apparel choices—as long as they are of high quality. Linen suits are not recommended. Sure, they look great on the hanger, but wrinkle easily and don't look crisp at the end of the day.

As for blouse fabrics, cotton and linen are generally the best choices. Silks, too, are quite acceptable and certainly fashionable. While these natural fibers generally test best, some high-quality synthetic fibers can also provide a polished addition to your wardrobe.

Blouses

➥ The color of your blouse has a definite impact on your overall look. As with suits, solid colors are the wisest wardrobe investments. While most blouse colors test well, choose tones to benefit the particular suit. For example, when wearing a light-colored suit, add an authoritative look with a dark or brightly colored blouse. Finally, always select blouses of high quality, colors, and styles that are complimentary to you.

Hosiery

Image consultants have found that women who wear hosiery in their own skin-tone portray a more conservative image than those who wear darker or colored stockings the majority of the time.

A good rule of thumb, then, is to stick with skin-toned hosiery—particularly if your company maintains a rigid corporate culture.

Once again, take a look around and see what your trusted colleagues are wearing. In some business environments (retail, for instance) colored hosiery may be perfectly acceptable. In most offices, however, your best bet is to go conservative.

Shoes

The classic pump generally works best in business. Again, heels should measure two to three inches in height. By investing in leather rather than synthetic materials, you will convey a more distinguished image. Recommended colors: navy, black, cordovan, and taupe.

Handbags/briefcases/portfolios

➥ It's always best to invest in leather accessories. Choose classic, rather than trendy, items. As with shoes, recommended colors are navy, black, cordovan, and taupe.

During my business etiquette seminars, I'm often asked

whether it's appropriate to carry both a purse and a briefcase. My answer is "yes," as long as the purse is a shoulder bag that is compact in appearance. Also, it should contain only necessary items (wallet, hair brush, basic cosmetics, etc.). If you have it packed full and it accidentally drops open, your life history could be revealed. This is definitely not advisable in a business setting.

Glasses

If you wear glasses, they should be both functional and complimentary, enhancing your facial features and contributing to the kind of image you wish to portray. Most eyewear facilities have well-qualified professionals to assist you. It is advisable, especially for women, to have more than one set of frames—something businesslike for working hours and something a little more casual for after-hours gatherings.

Regardless of the style(s) chosen, be sure to purchase clear, as opposed to tinted, lenses for use in the office. Since eye contact is of the utmost importance when communicating with others, your bright orbs should be highly visible, rather than hidden.

Jewelry

There's no doubt about it. Your choice of jewelry is a direct reflection of you. This can't be emphasized too much.

To play it safe, always choose jewelry that enhances your wardrobe. For example, when wearing a suit or dress with pearlized buttons, wear pearl earrings. Or when wearing a gold-tone necklace with a black suit, wear gold earrings with a black stone.

Earrings. Don't let dangling earrings drag you down the corporate ladder. Chandeliers are great in dining rooms and may serve you well on the social scene; but they definitely don't belong in an office setting. As with other pieces of jewelry, your safest bet is to choose those pieces that are simple yet elegant.

Watches. Besides being functional, the watch you wear is a valuable accessory item. That's why it's wise to invest in a classic style that blends well with both your business and after-hours attire. Image consultants have found that the tank style with black lizard or gold-tone band tests best.

The Rule of Thirteen

Seminar participants often ask, "How much jewelry is too much?" Or, "What about other accessories?" *The Rule of Thirteen* simplifies this mystery. After you dress in the morning, do a quick count of your accessories. Include the ornate buttons on your suit, dress, or blouse, the buckles on your shoes, your eyeglasses, scarf, and jewelry.

If the count is less than thirteen, you're probably well balanced in appearance. If you tally more than thirteen, play it safe and remove the unnecessary pieces.

Hair

Since your hair is often your most-noticed feature, invest in a hair style that is complimentary to your facial structure. Hair that is shoulder-length or shorter—or at least appears that way—gives the most professional appearance. So if you enjoy having hair shoulder-length or longer, pull it up or back in a style that gives you a chic look.

It goes without saying that hair color should appear natural. Beware of dark roots! Upkeep is the secret.

When splashing on perfume, keep in mind the old commercial jingle, "A little dab'll do you."

If someone is an arm's length away and comments on your perfume, you're probably wearing too much. Perfume should always be worn to make you—and those you allow to stand closer than an arm's length away—feel extra special.

Dress-down days

As noted in the previous chapter, the progressive nineties have brought a new wrinkle to the work place—dress-down days.

Although most companies who have instituted these lighten-up, dress-more-casually days generally issue a fairly specific set of guidelines, for women in particular the choices can be difficult.

Just how short can that casual skirt be? What about halter tops? Are "skorts" appropriate? And if so, must they be worn with a blouse, or is a tee shirt acceptable?

Again, your particular corporate climate will dictate what is appropriate. Look around and see what your female boss and trusted colleagues are wearing. For men, I suggest the following rule of thumb: When in doubt, ask.

Commonly Asked Questions About Image Tips for Women

Q. What kind of wardrobe does the term "business casual" imply?

A. For women, a casual dress may be worn—as long as it isn't too revealing. If the event is outdoors and the occasion merits, it may also be in order for women to wear a higher-quality pair of slacks or bermudas (rather than shorts) with a fashionable yet conservative top and matching shoes.

In recent years the "skort" has become a popular addition to women's wardrobes. Worn with a matching top and/or jacket, it can make a positive business fashion statement—in the appropriate environment, of course.

Q. I am a business woman who enjoys wearing earrings and I am considering getting my ears double-pierced. Do you think this will detract from my appearance?

A. Yes. While single piercing is acceptable, double piercing flirts with faddishness.

Q. I'm a secretary who recently received a briefcase as a birthday gift. Although I really like it, I'm hesitant to use it for fear of looking pretentious. Is carrying a briefcase appropriate for someone in my position?

A. Certainly! Briefcases are not limited to executives. They are an efficient way to transport paperwork. Use it, by all means.

Q. My colleague and I are having a friendly debate. She thinks wearing hosiery is essential during work hours. Since I have a tan, I don't think wearing hosiery is necessary. What is your opinion?

A. No matter what the season, hosiery should *always* be worn by women in a business environment. And that's a bare fact of professional life!

4.

Office Etiquette

How much time do you spend at work?

If you're like most people, you probably spend more waking hours on the job than you do at home. And also if you're like most workers, you probably treat your office and work place colleagues just a notch better than you do family members. Even so, it doesn't hurt to evaluate the way you treat your coworkers, employees, supervisors and other internal customers and clients. After all, these people are often just as vital to our success as our most important external customers and clients. This chapter has been designed to help you strengthen and enhance the work-place relationships you often take for granted.

Guest etiquette

When inviting guests to your office, observe the following code of behavior.

➤—0 Inform your receptionist of the visitor's expected arrival time. Be sure to include your guest's name and any special instructions. For example,

"I'm expecting John Smith about 10 a.m. When he arrives, please buzz me and I'll come out to greet him."

➤—0 Request that each guest sign in and wear a name tag. In this way, each company employee the guest encounters will be able to address him or her by name. Everyone appreciates that personal touch.

➤—0 When possible, greet your visitor personally in the reception area. When you're not able to do this, ask one of your staff members to greet and escort the person to your office.

➤—0 When someone else shows a guest to your office, walk out from behind your desk to greet the person and offer a handshake as a gesture of hospitality.

➤—0 After your welcome, show your guest where you'd like him or her to sit with a verbal request or a nonverbal gesture such as motioning your hand toward an available seat.

➤—0 Offer your visitor coffee or tea, unless one of your staff has already done so.

Honing in on your guest's five senses

You can assure that your guest will have a fully satisfying visit if you gear your behavior toward his or her five senses.

♦ *Seeing.* Establish eye contact with your visitor.

♦ *Touching.* Greet the person with a confident handshake and end your meeting in the same way.

♦ *Hearing.* Use the visitor's name during your greetings and a few times during your meeting.

♦ *Tasting.* Offer the person a beverage. Ask twice. Most people refuse the first time offer out of politeness.

♦ *Smelling.* Don't overwhelm your visitor with your favorite perfume/cologne. Wear only enough so that you, not your guest, are aware of your favorite scent.

Giving out-of-town guests the VIP treatment

Hosting out-of-town guests means much more than simply putting them on your calendar and waiting for their arrival. Part of your responsibility as host is to extend your hospitality even before your guests have left their home turf. Whether the expected guests are out-of-town customers, clients, colleagues, or suppliers, you can be certain of one thing: They will appreciate any advanced planning that will make their time away from home a pleasant experience. Here are three courtesy tips for giving your out-of-town guests the VIP treatment.

➤—0 Make up a travel package and send it to them in advance. Include a map of the area showing the location of your office or business in relation to the airport or freeway. List the travel times by car and cab and provide the name and telephone numbers of recommended hotels and motels in the area. Depending on the relationship you share with your guest(s), you may even want to make the necessary lodging accommodations.

➤—0 Alert your company receptionist to your guest's arrival. Encourage the receptionist to welcome the person by name (last name, of course).

＝0 When appropriate, circulate a memo to certain departments providing a brief description of the visitor's name, arrival date, and company affiliation and the purpose of the visit. In this way, employees will be able to make comfortable use of small talk should the opportunity for conversation take place.

Smoke signals

As you know, smoking is a hot topic in today's work place. Most office and businesses are eliminating decision making by establishing specific no-smoking policies and regulated smoking areas. Even with such directives, however, smoking remains a sensitive issue with many. So if you don't want your business potential to go up in a puff of smoke, it might behoove you to remember the following.

As a smoker . . .

♦ You have only one simple rule to follow: If you have even one nonsmoker in your midst, don't smoke! Having ashtrays available does *not* give a smoker an automatic license to light up.

♦ If you're in an office or setting that does not have ashtrays, the message should be clear. It is a non-smoking environment.

♦ If you're in a restaurant with people who say they don't mind if you light up, it is appropriate to smoke until the first course is served—provided, of course, that you're in the establishment's "smoking" section. If you must once again indulge your habit, wait until the last course, including dessert, has been removed.

As a non-smoker, you have definite rights. Here's how to exercise them with class.

♦ If a smoker is polite enough to ask if cigarette smoke bothers you, be courteous and say, "Thank you for asking. I would appreciate it if you didn't smoke."

♦ If you're running a meeting and the request is made, respect the smoker's need by saying, "If you'd like, we'll take a break during our meeting."

◆ If the smoker in your midst does *not* ask permission to light up, it's acceptable to ask diplomatically, "Would you mind not smoking?" If the smoker prefers *not* to comply with your request, either tolerate it for the time being or find another place to sit or stand.

Cardinal sins in the work place

In a survey conducted by Robert Half International, 50 percent of residents cited "criticizing an employee in front of others" as one of the most serious sins one could commit in a work environment. To avoid this and other transgressions, always observe the following half-percents.

➥ Never criticize an employee in front of others.

➥ Always give employees the opportunity to express themselves.

➥ Never be late for an appointment. Isn't it funny? Being on time is such a simple, basic concept. Then why do so many people have a problem with punctuality? If we all respected time as much as we respect space, no one would ever be late. With the frenzied pitch at which most of us go about our business dealings these days, punctuality is a big priority. The busier people are, the less tolerance they have for others' being late. Besides being rude, lateness can mean two strikes against you before your meeting even begins. Here are some tips to keep you on track.

◆ Set your watch early.

◆ When scheduling appointments, focus on the time you need to leave rather than the arrival time. By doing so, you will feel more in control of your time.

◆ If you're preparing to leave for a meeting or appointment, break the habit of doing just one more thing or accepting that last-minute phone call. Focus on the commitment you've made.

◆ Take pride in how others perceive you. Don't ruin your reputation by being late.

If you are often kept waiting by a chronically late business associate, there are a couple of things you can do. One is to confront this person with his or her time management problem. A second option is to try scheduling your meeting with this person fifteen minutes earlier than the actual starting time.

Dealing with interruptions

↳ Constant interruptions are not only distracting; they can put a damper on productivity. Unwelcome office interruptions can be handled in several ways. A simple yet sometimes impractical strategy is to close your door when you do not wish to be disturbed. This effectively puts a stop to any kind of interruption. If you'd rather keep your door open, or are located at an open-ended work station, consider repositioning your desk and/or work area. If your desk is now facing the entrance to your station, for example, turn it around so you won't see passers-by.

When a staff member or other visitor drops by to discuss something that could just as easily be taken up during a weekly work meeting or at a more convenient time, thank him or her for bringing the issue to your attention. Then let the person know you feel the topic could be better handled at another time or by your group as a whole and that the issue will be put on the appropriate agenda.

Let your staff members know that, while you welcome the chance to meet with them on a one-to-one basis, you would appreciate their scheduling a specific and more convenient time to do so. Tactfully explain to them that by scheduling an appointment, you will be able to give them your undivided attention and not feel pressured to squeeze in their concerns (which you consider very significant) among other matters.

If you are a manager, maintain an open-door policy for a given hour in the morning and in the afternoon. Encourage your staff to drop by during those times if the question or matter to be discussed will take ten minutes or less. If it appears the topic to be addressed will require more time, request that they schedule a meeting.

Meeting manners

Meetings matter! You'll be hard-pressed to find anyone to challenge that statement. Still, how many times have you found yourself in a meeting you feel is boring and unproductive? We all have. By the same token, we've all enjoyed well-planned, efficiently-run meetings that leave us with a sense of accomplishment and maybe even the enthusiasm we need to plunge forward.

To help ensure that every meeting you plan fits the latter description from now on, observe the following meeting manners.

↳ When announcing the meeting, state why it is being held.

➤⊸ Give each person a reason for being present. For example:

"Mary, would you prepare and present a five-minute summary of your department's weekly ideas?"

Even if you're inviting an employee whose role does not garner a listing on the official meeting agenda, be specific as to the importance of his or her presence. For example:

"John, we'll be discussing marketing strategies for the new book. Since you've been part of the project from its development stages, we'd like you to be present. Perhaps you'll have some fresh ideas we haven't considered."

➤⊸ Prepare a written agenda for attendees to follow. When possible, distribute the agenda a few days prior to the meeting.

➤⊸ Be early. Get to the meeting before anyone else arrives. By doing so, you'll be able to prepare the room, lay out the agendas (if they haven't already been distributed) and greet each attendee. You'll also set the tone for others to arrive promptly.

➤⊸ Begin the meeting on time. Even if only two of five expected attendees are present, get started. By doing so, you'll establish the reputation that you respect the time of others (and subtly imply that you expect the same courtesy).

➤⊸ State the purpose of the meeting.

➤⊸ Involve each person in attendance. This may be a formal involvement (such as calling for a summary that you have previously asked someone to prepare and present) or an informal gesture—like welcoming a new employee to the staff, observing an employee's anniversary with the company, or even paying a compliment to someone for a job well done.

➤⊸ Maintain control of the meeting. If someone digresses from the agenda, be tactful. Allow the person to finish speaking, summarize what has been said, and then diplomatically establish a time and place for the discussion to continue. For example:

"Let's make that topic a point of discussion for our next meeting." Or, *"Suzanne and Bob, would you like to form a committee to research that area further and present your findings during our next meeting?"*

➤⊸ At the conclusion of the meeting, summarize what has been discussed.

➤⊸ End the meeting promptly.

People will enjoy attending your meetings when they learn they can count on you to respect their time and talents.

Podium protocol

Introducing speakers is a real art—one that involves its own protocol. Here are some podium etiquette rules to help you present a polished image.

*—0 Be prepared. When scheduling speakers, request that biographical information in the form of an introductory paragraph be sent to you ahead of time. Practice what you're planning to say so that your remarks appear natural, extemporaneous, and conversational.

*—0 After introducing the speaker, wait until the person nears the podium. Then step back and welcome him or her with a handshake.

*—0 Following the speech, return to the podium and extend your thanks to the person once again with another handshake and a verbal acknowledgment made through the microphone.

*—0 If several people will be speaking and you are to introduce each of them, thank the person who just spoke before presenting the next person.

Cafeteria courtesies

Just as there are rules and codes of behavior for the working areas of offices and businesses, so too with the cafeteria. Here are some social mores for cafeteria dining.

*—0 Keep the line moving. Read the list of specials before it's your turn to order. Then you won't run the risk of holding up the line.

*—0 Treat cafeteria workers with respect. They are human beings, not slaves, and are due the same courtesy you extend your clients and customers.

*—0 Don't force yourself on senior management. If the higher-ups wish you to join them, they will extend the invitation. If and when you are the recipient of such an invitation, never bring up information that may not be company knowledge (especially personal information about fellow employees) or topics that should be reserved for discussion at a scheduled meeting.

*—0 Avoid making your lunch gathering look like the company clique. Rather than dining with the same people each day, be sociable and sit with different colleagues periodically, or invite others to join your table.

*—0 Don't make derogatory remarks about the food. After all, you're not the company nutritionist.

➥ Be sociable. Rather than sitting alone reading a book, use this time to get to know employees from other departments or to become better acquainted with your coworkers. Aside from the obvious social growth of such contact, you never know when such networking will pay off in a professional sense.

➥ Leave your eating area in the same condition you leave your work area at the end of the day. (We hope the operative word here is *neat*.) The only trace of your presence that should be left behind is a good impression and memories of the pleasantries you have exchanged with others during this break from work.

Savvy with supervisors

No matter how much you might feel as if you've entered another realm when you interact with your supervisors, from a business etiquette standpoint there is no such thing as VIP protocol. If you observe the same business etiquette and extend the same courtesies you do with your coworkers, clients, customers, suppliers, and anyone else with whom you have business dealings, you won't have any concerns.

Asking for a raise

One issue that might require some forethought and planning on your part, however, is approaching a supervisor for a raise.

We've all been involved in a situation like this. We love our work. We don't even mind putting in extra hours. However, we feel we deserve more money for our efforts. How do we approach our supervisor without ruffling his or her feathers?

➥ Since raises are generally based on an individual's performance record, here are some things to think about before approaching the powers-that-be: Have you been asked to assume more responsibility? If so, what kind? Have you improved your company's bottom line to the extent that your supervisor would acknowledge that you deserve a raise? If you're able to answer "yes" to either of these questions, prepare a summary report. List specific achievements to support your belief that you deserve a raise. Then schedule a meeting with your supervisor.

Be word-wise

➥ Though popular movie and TV hits might lead us to believe that the use of four-letter words has become commonplace, don't be fooled. Vulgar language has never been—nor will it ever be—acceptable in a business environment. An occasional "hell" or "damn" is tolerable to most people. But anything beyond that is strictly taboo. If you're guilty of this breech of business etiquette, start working now to clean up your vocabulary. If you're confronted by someone who uses profanity, on the other hand, you have two choices: ignore the behavior or walk away from it. Whatever you do, don't lower yourself by falling into the same bad habit.

When you're let go
The closing years of the twentieth century will go down in history as the era of corporate mergers and acquisitions.

Unfortunately, during these transactions, which were designed for the growth of many companies, numerous employees who gave ten, twenty-five, or more years of dedicated services to their organizations suddenly found themselves taken by the hand and led right out the front door. It seemed their reward for getting to the office early, staying late, and making personal sacrifices was to be let go under the guise of "corporate restructuring."

Of course, no one wants to be part of a situation like this. If and when it happens, however, here are five principles of etiquette to help you react in a professional and mature manner.

➲ Don't let your emotions overrule your good sense. Maintain your professionalism at all times.

➲ Never burn bridges behind you. Follow up any telephone calls or correspondence received, always remembering the first admonition to keep your professional cool.

➲ When discussing the matter with others, be as positive as possible. Focus on the "good" years and direct conversation to the future.

➲ Rather than placing yourself in a compromising position, remember that in many instances, silence can indeed be golden. This may be one of those instances.

➲ Be ready to seize and act upon any opportunities that may appear. Keeping yourself in a positive frame of mind will ensure that you are always prepared to present a professional and polished image to any potential employer.

Commonly Asked Questions About Office Etiquette

> Q. Some of my employees need assistance with the definition of "nine to five." A few of our new hires arrive at the office at 8:58 a.m., say their good mornings, and

then get something to drink.

By the time they are in their work areas, it's 9:15 a.m. They're young, they're naive, and they don't seem to equate starting times with productivity. How can I diplomatically let them know that they are expected to begin work at 9:00 a.m. *sharp*?

A. As their manager, either tell them directly through a memo or address this matter during a meeting in which they are present. If your company has a policy and procedures manual, perhaps a section addressing this point should be added.

Q. One of my employees thinks nothing of making and accepting personal telephone calls during the work day. She doesn't seem to realize that she is getting paid to work rather than make idle chit-chat with her friends.

I've discussed this situation with her, but she continues to make and accept these calls between conversations with customers. How can I get it into her head that time is money?

A. Perhaps the person you describe doesn't realize that she is, in essence, "stealing" time from the company. Since you've already brought this to her attention verbally and haven't seen any change, I suggest you document her actions in writing (which can also act as a written warning).

If your telephone system can provide a printout of outgoing and incoming calls from and to this person's phone line, bring to her attention the number of minutes or hours she spends in personal conversations. If you continue to see little or no improvement, try docking her pay. That should take care of it!

Q. One of my employees has the habit of continually looking at his watch during meetings. I find this very offensive. How can I keep him from offending customers with the same action?

A. Make this person aware of this annoying habit in private. Discuss the ramification of his actions with him and recommend that he either break the habit or remove his watch before entering the meeting.

Q. How can I handle someone who comes into my office and interrupts me when I'm speaking on the phone? People in our office act as though—by virtue of their physical presence—their business should precede that of the person with whom I'm conversing by phone.

   When I explain that I am in the middle of a conversation, I frequently hear, "This will just take a second"—and the person continues to talk. I'm faced with the choice of being rude either to the person on the phone or to the person in my office.

A. Without a doubt, the person on the phone should be given precedence. Try closing your office door to avoid these invasions of privacy. If you're in a work station without a door, don't make eye contact with others when you don't want to be interrupted.

Q. I was recently promoted to a management position and now oversee staff members who were previously my peers. How can I get them to work with me?

A. ▬● The best advice I can give is to follow the golden rule: treat them as respectfully as you would like be treated. Also, recognize that your staff is made up of individuals with separate needs. By demonstrating care for your employees' individuality, you'll receive more from them collectively.

Q. How do you react to a person who consistently shows up twenty to twenty-five minutes early for appointments?

A. When scheduling the appointment, let the early bird know that you'll be in another meeting until ten minutes before you are scheduled to meet. By making this point ahead of time, you won't feel as if you're keeping this person waiting when he or she shows up ahead of time.

Q. Some of my colleagues show the most amazing insensitivity at meetings. They think nothing of talking with each other while someone else is speaking. A few of them even use nail clippers during a meeting!

A. For those who exhibit rude behavior by carrying on

their own conversations while someone else is speaking, here are some tricks from seasoned presenters. If you're the speaker, simply stop dead in your verbal tracks, glance over at the offenders, and maintain eye contact until they quiet down. Then resume speaking. If you're not the speaker, try directing a glance (maybe even a glare) to the offenders. Eventually they should get the point.

As for the frustrated manicurists . . . after the first clip, pause; glance at the nail clipper (the object, not the person) for a fixed moment; then continue. Although you may not see immediate results, there's a good chance the person will get the point.

Q. I work for three people: two lawyers and one office services manager. One of the lawyers I report to is second in command at our firm. Since he is frequently out of the office, he expects me, his administrative assistant, to provide him with a report on "what goes on" when he is out of the office.

My problem is this. The other lawyer I report to slacks off when our boss is gone. I do not feel, however, that it is my place to "rat" on this person. My boss has told me that it is my responsibility to be loyal by explaining what goes on (or doesn't go on) when he is out.

I have worked for this boss for twelve years and love my job. I believe that I am loyal to him. However, I feel that he is out of line by putting me in this compromising situation. What do you think?

A. Have you ever heard the saying, "When you point a finger at someone, he will point two fingers at you?"

Professionalism is the word at all costs—even if it means not being the spy your boss would like you to be.

Q. A member of my staff consistently mispronounces words and abuses the English language and I'm concerned about the impression this makes on our clients. I'd like to get him to break the habit and am planning to meet with him to discuss the matter. Am I handling the situation properly?

A. It sounds like it. Encourage him to practice, practice, practice. Let him know that you have his best interests at heart and that you don't want his poor command of the language to keep him from being promotable. Of course, as you seem to know already, you should never correct his mistakes in public. That would be bad manners on your part.

Q. Is there a tactful way to ask the people in my office to pitch in for a gift for a coworker?

A. I recommend that you let the people in your office know that a gift is being purchased collectively. Invite each person to join in by mentioning a dollar figure range (for example, $5 to $10). Be sure to give them a deadline for getting the money to you.

Q. My boss called me into his office last week to give me a company bonus. Besides thanking him verbally, is a written thank-you in order?

A. Yes. By displaying your appreciation, you'll be demonstrating both your sincerity and an attention to detail.

Q. Our company doesn't permit employees to accept gifts from suppliers. I'm a marketing manager and have been sent some holiday gifts from a few of our current suppliers. Is there a polite way to refuse these presents?

A. While I understand the reason for your company's policy, it's worth noting that suppliers give business-related gifts as a token of appreciation, not as a bribe. The best thing for you to do, under the circumstances, is to thank him for his thoughtfulness, but be "up-front" and explain your company's policy.

Q. I am in the midst of getting a divorce. Once it is finalized, I would like my colleagues and customers to begin calling me by my birth name. How can I tactfully request this?

A. Since most people are creatures of habit, be tolerant of those who may not immediately conform to your request. Meanwhile, here are some suggestions for establishing a different last name.

➤ Request that your name change be made on paperwork. This can generally be accomplished by working through your supervisor or your company's personnel department.

➤ Request that your supervisor begin referring to you in memos by your birth name.

➤ Begin signing correspondence with your new (old) name.

In time, your colleagues and clients will catch on.

5.

Business Greetings and Introductions

🢤 **Make the first ten words count!**
Do you want to get someone's attention? In a positive sense, of course. Then use his or her name.

Remember the four rules presented in chapter 1? Nothing captures a person's attention more positively and more quickly than saying his name. That's why I encourage you to try to work the name of the person you are addressing into the first several words you speak.

This rule goes hand in hand with the suggestion that you use a form of thanks in the first ten or twelve words.

"Thank you for taking the time to meet with me today, John."

If you're saying to yourself, "I usually do that," congratulations! You already know how effective it can be. The key is to condition yourself to observe this half-percent all the time.

The five commandments
While you won't see these "commandments" carved in stone, they are of vital importance in greetings and introductions. So it will behoove you to heed them.

🢤 **Stand up.** When you are seated and someone approaches you to say "hello" with a handshake, stand up, whether you are a man or woman. By doing so, you show the person you are greeting that you are giving him or her your full attention.

🢤 What if you're scrunched in a booth or in another situation that makes it difficult or impossible to stand up? Then do the bob. In other words, simply make an effort to stand. When you do so, the person who has approached you will probably motion to you to stay seated. At least, let's hope so!

The question of gender and standing comes up often in my seminars because of past cultural mores. Once upon a time, when women were seen almost exclusively in the social arena, it was not considered necessary for them to stand. Today men and women interact in the business world on the same professional levels, and women should act accordingly.

What if a business woman is attending a social function with her spouse or significant other? Is standing still in order? By all means! This anecdote should illustrate why. A few years ago I attended a gathering with a male friend. Several of his clients were present. I knew none of these people. As my friend introduced me to each, I took note. If I remained seated during the introduction, I was greeted with a handshake and a "Nice to meet you." When, however I made the effort to stand, I was greeted with a handshake, a "nice to meet you" *and*, within a few minutes, "What kind of work do you do?"

It verified a point I had been making in my seminars. Standing when shaking hands demonstrates you've been there before.

Make eye contact. The importance of this rule can't be overemphasized. Looking someone directly in the eye will accomplish three things: You will project an image of self-confidence and a healthy self-esteem, you will be perceived as a good listener, and you will probably receive the same courtesy when you speak.

Smile. It sends others a message of acceptance. A smile really *is* worth a thousand words—maybe even more.

When I see someone smiling at others, I see a person with self-confidence, a person with the self-assurance needed to greet and accept others with finesse and poise. And that, trust me, is a real asset in many circles—but particularly in the business realm.

Say your name. If you're meeting someone for the first time, it's a given: Introduce yourself using your first and last name. If you have met the person previously but suspect he or she may not remember your name, eliminate potential embarrassment by reintroducing yourself. You might say something like, "I'm Rebecca Johnson. We met at last year's conference. It's so nice to see you again." Even if the person does not remember your name, you have provided the perfect opportunity for a little fudging with a response like, "Certainly I remember you, Rebecca. It is good to see you again."

╺╾0 **Shake hands.** Touching and patting don't cut it. Stick with a handshake. And while we're on that subject, please note: There are firm handshakes and there are FIRM handshakes. Seminar participants often ask, "How firm should a handshake be? And how long should it last?" Generally speaking, a handshake should last only as long as it takes to greet the person. It should be firm enough to display your sense of confidence without being a bonecrusher. If you're shaking hands with someone whose body weight is much less than yours, then lighten up! Guaranteed—the person will appreciate your consideration.

For more on the gender issues involved in shaking hands, see chapter 15, Men and Women as Colleagues.

Basic pointers for meetings and greetings

Men:

╺╾0 Don't wait for a woman to initiate a handshake.

╺╾0 Always offer the woman your full hand in a handshake. Forget the business of shaking fingers. Offer your full hand.

╺╾0 Offer a confident handshake to men and women alike.

╺╾0 Avoid the "my hand over your hand" handshake, as this can be interpreted as a subtle form of one-upmanship.

Women:

╺╾0 Always offer a complete and firm handshake.

╺╾0 Stand when shaking hands.

╺╾0 Shake hands with customers and clients, even when you meet them outside the work place.

╺╾0 Never stay behind the desk when meeting or greeting someone. When shaking hands, the only thing that should be between the two of you is space.

╺╾0 Shake hands at both the beginning and the end of a meeting.

╺╾0 Give a handshake indicative of the confident, self-assured person you are.

╺╾0 Avoid wearing an oversized ring on the right hand. It

can hinder others from giving you a firm handshake.

Be an easy person to meet and greet. Just observe the following:
    •—0 Keep your right hand free.
    •—0 If you're asked to prepare your own name tag, be sure to print your name (especially your first name) in large, legible letters.
    •—0 When wearing a name tag, place it on your right side. That way, those shaking hands with you will be able to glance down at your name tag (rather than looking across) as you are introducing yourself. When the person with whom you're shaking hands has to break eye contact with you for more than a second or two, either she will not take time to look at your name or she will appear shifty-eyed. The simple little right-side trick eliminates this awkwardness.

Commonly Asked Questions About Greetings and Introductions

Q. When I am introducing my female supervisor to a male customer, whose name should I say first?

A. •—0 Man or woman, the customer's name should always be said first. Business introductions should be based on rank rather than gender.

Q. How can you tell whether someone wants to be called by his or her first, rather than last, name?

A. •—0 Here's how to gauge your decision. If the person is a few layers above you from an organizational structure standpoint, or closer to your parents' ages than yours, using the last name may be the best choice. If the person ranks closer to your level or is closer to you in age, his or her first name may be used. If you have any doubt, use the last name. You can't get into trouble being too formal. You may, however, leave a negative impression if you're too casual.

Q. When addressing a woman by her last name, should I use "Ms.," "Miss" or "Mrs."?

A. •—0 "Ms." is most accepted. Note: If you say the "s" of "Ms." softly enough you will sound $66\frac{2}{3}$ percent right because it sounds so much like "Miss."

Q. When addressing a group of business women, is it appropriate to refer to them as "ladies," "women," or "female"?

A. When business women were asked this question in a recent study, most preferred the term "women."

Q. Is it ever appropriate for people to introduce themselves and include the forms of "Ms.," "Mrs." or "Mr." in their names?

A. Never. The few people who mistakenly do this appear to bestow honorifics upon themselves. They come off sounding like someone afflicted with Capital P Syndrome—Pretentiousness!

Q. When in doubt, is it acceptable to ask whether you may address someone by his or her first name?

A. No. if you ask for permission to use someone's first name, you may be placing that person in an awkward situation. Use the person's last name a few times during the conversation. This opens the door for a response like, "Please call me Jim."

Q. What's the best way to handle that embarrassing situation of being approached by someone whose name slips your mind?

A. ▬◐ Initiate a handshake and reintroduce yourself. In most cases the person will do likewise.

Q. What should I do when someone calls me by the wrong name?

A. ▬◐ It depends. If you're going to be with the person for just a brief moment, let it go. If, however, your meeting is expected to last for a while, simply restate your name. In such a case, diplomacy is definitely in order. For example, say the person incorrectly calls you Bob. You might respond, "I'm sorry. It's Rob." Or perhaps your name is Marian and the person calls you Mary Ann. You could say, "People frequently call me Mary Ann. But I prefer Marian."

Q. What is the best way to deal with names that are difficult to pronounce?

A. ⊶ When meeting someone who has such a name, ask the person to pronounce it for you. Then say it yourself. If possible, write the name down, using both the correct spelling and its phonetic equivalent. This will assist you in pronouncing it correctly the next time you use it.

Q. I'm so tired of being called "Kathy." My name is "Kathleen" and I prefer that to the nickname. How should I tactfully deal with people who shorten my name?

A. The next time you're called "Kathy," immediately respond, "I'm sorry. It's Kathleen." By using a form of apology as you're correcting the person, you'll spare his or her ego.

Q. It is very common for several people from the same company to tour our facility in a group. When my supervisor is giving such a tour, he frequently shows customers through our department. When I am introduced to as many as five or more persons during this "walk through," is it still appropriate for me to initiate a handshake with each of them?

A. ⊶ Let your sixth sense be your guide. While handshakes may be in order, a simple smile and a nod may be enough to make the visitors feel welcome. Often the decision will depend on the pace at which the group is moving through your facility.

Q. I suffer from sweaty palms. When shaking hands, I'm never sure if it's better to apologize for my "condition" or to say nothing. What do you suggest?

A. Before shaking hands, you may want to inconspicuously pat your hands on the side of your clothing. In reality, you're probably more aware of your "condition" than anyone else will be.

Q. After introducing myself to someone, how can I keep the person from invading my territory? When people stand too close to me, I become distracted and don't absorb everything the person is saying.

A. ⊶ Most people need their space. Until you have established rapport with someone, it's best to maintain a
distance of two arm lengths. Thus, after shaking hands,
simply maintain the same distance between you as during the handshake.

When a person begins invading your territory, try
to back up. If you find that you've backed yourself into
a wall, simply turn yourself slightly (just a fraction of a
turn, so as not to appear rude) away from the person.
By doing this, you'll feel more in control of your space.

Q. Is there ever a time when introductions are *not* necessary?

A. Introductions may not be necessary when you're talking with someone and another person approaches to
say *hello*. If it's not a good time for the newcomer to
break into the conversation, simply excuse yourself,
break out of the conversation for a moment and acknowledge the person through eye contact, a smile, or a
quick handshake. By not introducing the two people,
you're giving a subtle cue that the newcomer should
move on.

6.

The Art of Business Conversation

Many people believe themselves to be good conversationalists because they talk a lot. They're mistaken.

In reality, a good conversationalist does as much listening as speaking—maybe more. The real strength of such a person lies in the ability to draw others into the discussion. It all falls under the category of verbal communication—one of your greatest professional tools. To put it succinctly, the art of business conversation includes knowing what to say and when to say it. It also includes the ability to recognize when to listen. You too can develop these essential business skills.

How to start and sustain a conversation

Have you ever been obliged to attend a function at which you knew no one? As you approached people or as they approached you, what did you talk about?

Believe it or not, it's quite easy to start and sustain a conversation. The key is to listen more than you speak. Just as important as knowing what to ask is recognizing how to phrase questions. A sure way to get others to respond is to ask open-ended questions. If, for example, you've just met someone, don't ask, "Are you one of Bill Jones' customers?" This is a dead-end question likely to get you little more than a "yes" or a "no" in response. Instead, use an interrogative—Who? What? When? Where? Why? How? For example, "How do you know Bill Jones?" This kind of question should get you a response with some detail, thus opening the door to more conversation.

While it's important to phrase and position your questions

carefully, it's also crucial that you appear to be sincerely interested in what you are asking the person and in the response elicited. Rather than trying to bluff your way through, work on developing a sincere interest in others. Everyone knows you can spot a phony a mile away.

How to be perceived as a good listener

Using interrogatives to open questions is only the beginning of getting a good conversation off the ground. The other part of a healthy and productive conversation is letting the person you're talking to know that you are truly listening.

In addition to simply opening your ears and eliminating distractions, there are a few techniques guaranteed to help you develop your listening skills.

Take two. Have you ever started talking before the other person was finished speaking? An effective way to avoid a head-on conversation collision is to count to two after a person has finished talking.

Jump on the same wavelength. Learn to identify people as auditory, visual, or feeling and then communicate with them in their own language. An auditory person, for instance, will often have background music playing and will consistently use works like *sounds, talk, tell, hear,* and *tone.* A visual person typically communicates best with the aid of charts, maps, and other visuals and sprinkles his vocabulary with words like *perceive, look, imagine, observe, view,* and *see.* A feeling person, who frequently likes to juggle many tasks at once, gravitates to words like *empathize, feel, understand, sense,* and the like. Pick up on these cues and learn to speak the language.

Paraphrase. A sure way to let others know you heard what they said is by paraphrasing or reiterating. When you can paraphrase while on the same wavelength, you'll really be perceived as a good listener.

If you're able to identify the person as *auditory,* for instance, paraphrase what you heard by saying something like, "It *sounds* like . . ." or, "I *heard* you say that . . ." If you are able to identify the person who just spoke as *visual,* paraphrase what you just heard by using phrases like, "I *see* that . . ." or, "It *appears* that . . ." or, "It *looks* like . . ." Finally, if you are able to identify the person who spoke as *feeling*, paraphrase what you heard using such terms as "I *understand* that . . ." or, "I *feel* that . . ."

One of the beauties of this follow-up listening is that the person you're talking to will probably be more attentive to what you say, as well.

Small, medium, and large talk
Different situations call for different levels of conversation.

➤─◗ **Small talk.** This is simply conversation about everyday happenings—the weather, sports, your immediate environment, etc. The advantage of making small talk is that everyone is able to participate. Thus when establishing rapport with someone, begin with small talk.

Medium talk. Medium talk deals with information specific to a group. For example, two people may make medium talk by discussing the company they represent. Although the others at their table may be familiar with the company being discussed, they may not be able to participate in the conversation.

Large talk. Large talk deals with very specific information. For example, let's say six people work for the same company—three in sales and three in accounting.

If the three people from the sales department begin discussing their monthly quotas, or the three individuals in the accounting department begin talking about a new accounting software package, each group is making large talk. They are making conversation understood or of interest to a limited number of persons.

When not to talk
➤─◗ When you're involved in conversation with others, a good rule of thumb for talking about yourself or your affiliations is to do so only when asked a question.

➤─◗ If you know nothing about the topic under discussion (someone may be making medium or large talk), remain silent.

How to participate in a conversation without talking
Believe it or not, you can participate in a conversation by saying absolutely nothing. Just maintain your role as an active listener.

Make use of your body language. Maintain eye contact. Smile. Nod. You'll be a welcome part of the conversation without ever opening your mouth.

Let your gestures speak for you

▼─0 Body language and receptivity are vitally important aspects of animated and interesting dialogue. When participating in a conversation, be sure to project a positive and friendly attitude. Smile. Touch with a handshake. Maintain eye contact. Nod. And keep an open mind. Even if you are not all that interested in the person with whom you are speaking, keep an open mind regarding future relationships. It's a good way to help develop your professional network. You never know when your paths will cross again.

How to gain control of a conversation

▼─0 Be open and friendly.

▼─0 Take risks.

▼─0 Be the first to say "hello."

▼─0 Be genuinely interested in people. They'll be flattered and interested in you.

▼─0 Be open to new ideas.

▼─0 Accept people as they are.

All of these half-percents can give you the competitive edge in conversations and in life. Work on developing these attributes. You have nothing to lose and everything to gain.

How to change the subject—tactfully

Have you ever felt stuck in a conversation and unsure how to get out of it? Perhaps you continued to lend an ear, eagerly awaiting a break in the dialogue (or monologue) so you could change the subject or escape.

▼─0 When you find yourself in such a situation, whatever you do, be tactful. If, for instance, you want to change the subject, use lead-ins like,

"I heard you mention earlier . . ."

"You seem to know a lot about . . ."

If you're looking for an escape hatch, try something like,

"Before this meeting ends, I'd like to . . ."

"I see it's already 3 p.m. and . . ."

However you wrangle out of the conversation or change the subject, avoid being offensive or insulting to anyone.

Commonly Asked Questions About Business Conversation

Q. I work in a high-rise office complex and frequently find myself waiting for the elevator. When someone who is not my professional "equal" (a supervisor or manager, for instance) approaches, am I out of order in initiating a conversation? Or is this expected of me? I'm always confused in this situation.

A. A smile and a nod are always in order. Let the supervisor take it from there.

Q. I am annoyed when people try to finish a sentence for me. Should I show my annoyance or just let it go?

A. Sometimes overly enthusiastic people think they're helping by filling in the blank for you. In reality, they're stepping on your sentences. To help break them of this annoying habit in a graceful manner, wait until the person has completed your sentence for you. Then pause briefly and complete the sentence yourself as you would have done before the interruption.

Q. When visiting clients, I usually try to make small talk by referencing a photo on the desk, a print on the wall, or anything else that might break the ice. The problem is that the conversation sometimes goes on longer than I feel it should (particularly when I'm in a time crunch). How can I get the conversation back on track without appearing to take too much control?

A. Rather than be too bold or abrupt, wait for a slight pause and then take out your notebook. This is a gentle, inoffensive way to let the other person know you're ready to get down to business.

Q. What is the correct way to approach a group of people when they are already engaged in conversation?

A. Try making eye contact with one or more of the members of the group. After joining them, be sure to act as a listener, rather than trying to dominate the conversation.

Q. Is there a tactful way to interrupt someone who isn't talking *to* you, but *at* you? People who do this don't give you a chance to get a word in edgewise. What should I do the next time this happens?

A. Try some nonverbal techniques to break off the monologue. For example, break eye contact with the person. Or if you're sitting, lean slightly forward and glance at your watch. If necessary, you can interrupt by saying, "I heard you mention earlier . . . which reminds me . . ."

Q. After working as a systems analyst for more than fifteen years, I decided to raise a family. I've chosen to stay at home with our daughter for a few years. When entertaining my husband's clients and their spouses, I am often asked, "What do you do?" How can I respond without making "staying home" sound like such menial work?

A. Raising a family is, by far, the most important, challenging, difficult, and never-ending job in this world. It sounds as though you may be more sensitive to your answer than those asking the questions.

When people ask, "What do you do?" they may simply be trying to make conversation. The next time you're asked this question, try responding in one of the following ways:

"*I've chosen to stay home with our daughter.*"
"*I'm a domestic engineer.*"
"*I'm learning to be an early childhood specialist.*"
Whatever you say, do so with pride.

7.

Telephone Etiquette—How Phonogenic Are You?

Can you imagine working without a telephone? Can you imagine *living* without one?

Of all the communication devices we have available today, the telephone remains the form most widely used for contacting the outside world. With telephone communication increasingly complicated by such high-tech devices as beepers, voice mail, and car phones, a whole new phone etiquette has evolved. This chapter will bring you up to date on the latest in communication protocol.

How do you answer the phone?

Many people answer the phone haphazardly. Some identify themselves with first names; some (especially former military personnel) with last; others, with both. And some don't bother to identify themselves at all. You may even hear an occasional "Yo!" or "Yeah!" from the McManners generation.

In developing appropriate phone-answering skills, it's important to remember that the words you choose set the tone for the conversation that follows. So it's always to your benefit to choose the words that will get your conversation off to a good start.

Answering company phones

As some people already know, but nearly not enough recognize, your company receptionist is one of the most important people on your staff. Why? Because he or she is the gatekeeper for every single call that goes through your switchboard. What your receptionist says and how he or she says it are instrumental in the way your company or business is perceived by customers and clients, potential customers and clients, suppliers, and virtually anyone who, for whatever reason, has dialed your number.

For this reason, I always recommend that a telephone greeting begin with "Good morning" or "Good afternoon." Following should be a company name and, preferably, the name of the person who answered the phone. For example:

"Good morning! Customer service. This is Mary."

Be thorough but compact. Avoid reciting a litany. Callers, especially long-distance ones, despise lengthy greetings.

How your company phone should be answered

If you're an employee, there is only one way to answer the company phone—the way the company recommends you answer it.

If you've never been requested to answer the line in a particular fashion, perhaps now is the time to ask for directives.

In a large office setting, consistency is particularly important. What you say when answering the phone, therefore, should be based on the same format others use when answering their phones. By using the same style, you and your colleagues will project a sense of team spirit and professionalism.

Answering internal calls

If you can tell by the ring of your phone that an incoming call is internal, then it's appropriate to answer, "This is John." If you work for a large corporation and frequently receive telephone calls from individuals you hardly know, answer the line using both your first and last names.

Answering external calls

☛ Whenever you can tell by the ring of the phone that an incoming call is external, answer with both your first and last names.

"Good morning! Weiss Graphics. This is Mary Smith."

By identifying yourself this way, you project both responsibility and authority. Those who answer the phone using their first names only, by contrast, run the risk of being perceived as having responsibility without authority. It's one of those little business subtleties.

When you can't tell

How do you answer a call when you can't determine beforehand whether it's internal or external? Just assume it is external and identify yourself using both your first and last names.

Placing a call

Good telephone manners require that you identify yourself when placing a call.

"Good afternoon, this is Mary Smith of Weiss Graphics calling. Is Mr. Jones available?"

This will relieve the receptionist or whoever answers of that burdensome question, "Whom shall I say is calling?"

When you do reach Mr. Jones, don't just jump into the conversation. Be courteous and ask whether he has time to talk. Mr. Jones will appreciate your respect for his time.

Finally, a word about wrong numbers. Everyone misdials occasionally. When this happens to you, rather than simply hanging up without an explanation, apologize.

"I'm sorry; I must have misdialed."

Of course, as the recipient of a wrong number, you should always treat the misdialer graciously. Don't compound his or her embarrassment by a display of irritability at being interrupted.

Handling the most dreaded chore

Placing calls for a supervisor is generally looked upon with about as much enthusiasm as washing windows. That's probably because most people perceive having a secretary place his or her boss's calls as pretentious. Thank goodness this practice is generally the exception rather than the rule.

As affected as it may seem, the dreaded chore of placing calls for your supervisor can be handled with skill and finesse. Just follow these tips.

➥ Before placing the call, let your supervisor know that you are about to do so. He or she can then be ready to take the call, should the person be in.

➥ After reaching the person's office, explain the reason for your call. As soon as you have made contact, let your boss know that he or she can pick up the line immediately.

➥ If the person you are attempting to reach is not available, leave a message that "Mr. Smith, with XYZ Company, has phoned". Besides leaving your office number, I generally recommend that you also indicate when Mr. Smith can be reached.

When a call needs to be returned
When you're not available to accept a telephone call, it should be returned as soon as possible. For some that may mean ten minutes; for others, two days. Return EVERY call, or delegate the task to a staff member. Returning calls promptly can pay big dividends.

Getting others to return your calls—promptly
➼ When phoning someone who is not available to take your call, explain when and where you can be reached. The more specific you are, the more professional you will appear to your colleagues.

If you're calling long-distance, be sure to say so. Often your call will be accepted more readily when you mention this fact.

Winning at telephone tag
One of our culture's most frequently played games, telephone tag, can be very frustrating. Studies have shown that your chance of reaching the person you're calling on the first attempt is about one in six. These findings also indicate you could waste more than two years of your life playing telephone tag. Here are some courtesy tips designed to help you save time when communicating by phone.

➼ When talking to someone with whom you need to follow up, schedule a specific time for the next call.

➼ If the person you're trying to reach is not available, explain the reason for the call. Be specific. Someone else may be able to assist you.

➼ Be courteous to administrative personnel. Ask for their advice as to a convenient time to call back.

➼ When telephone communication seems to be going nowhere fast, look for alternatives. Drop the person a note or a fax.

Tips for telephone communication
Just as you prepare for face-to-face meetings, it's also advisable to prepare for phone calls that you are expecting to have returned. Here are three tips for displaying telephone aplomb.

➼ Before answering the phone, turn away from your other work.

➼ Smile when you answer the phone. Even though he or

she can't see you do so, your caller will feel as though you are genuinely interested in receiving the call.

    ──0 Let the other person speak without interruption. A sure way to keep yourself from interrupting is to use the pause rule we discussed earlier. Simply pause or count to two after the person finishes.

On hold

Have you ever met anyone who enjoyed being put on hold? I haven't. Unfortunately, there are times when it's necessary to employ this tiresome device.

    When you must put someone on hold, be sure it's for a good reason, such as needing time to pull the person's file or answer another line. Ask the person whether he or she will hold and then wait for a response, rather than just assuming that you will hear a "yes."

How long is too long?

How long can you put someone on hold without committing a social or business gaffe? Generally speaking, no longer than thirty to sixty seconds. When you're pulling a file or answering another line, thirty to sixty seconds seems to fly by. When, however, a caller is listening to dead silence, company propaganda, or a radio station he or she doesn't like, that short time can seem like an eternity. Be considerate.

Lowering defenses

When getting back on the line, reopen the conversation with a, "Thank you for holding, Mr. Jackson." By this courtesy you will let Mr. Jackson know you were aware that he was kind enough to give up his time.

How to handle a chatty caller

Have you ever found yourself on the phone with an overly talkative person, and wondered how to end the call without damaging the person's ego? Obviously, gentleness and tact are in order. When returning a call to a loquacious person, preface your conversation by saying something like, "I wanted to get back to you before leaving for my 2 p.m. meeting." With luck, the chatty one will realize you're operating under a time constraint. If, however, you're already involved in a conversation that appears to have no stopping point, wait for a pause and try ending the call with something like, "Well, I won't take any more of your time . . ." or, "Thanks for taking the time to talk. I know you must be busy, so . . ."

Call screening

Have you stopped to think that phone calls would never have to be screened if people would simply identify themselves when placing a call? It's so simple. Many people are so preoccupied trying to reach the other person, however, that it often doesn't cross their minds to identify themselves. Since we can't change everyone's habits, it's good to have a procedure in place to handle such situations. Here's what I suggest.

First tell the caller the whereabouts of the person requested, then ask for an identification. For example:

"Mr. Smith is in a meeting this morning. May I take your name and number and ask him to call you when he returns this afternoon?"

If the person is in, respond with something like,

"Let me put you through to Ms. Smith. And your name, please?"

With this kind of approach, you may say to yourself, If I accept calls from every Tom, Dick and Harry, I'll never get my work done!" While there may sometimes be an element of truth in such a stance, accessibility is the name of the game in business today. Many people try to emphasize their importance by being discriminatory about which calls to accept. Many opportunities have been lost by those who act in this manner. As the late Sam Walton, founder of the highly successful Wal-Mart chain, said in his book *Made In America*, "You have to think small to grow big." Even if you're the owner of a multimillion dollar business today, you had to start somewhere; and it was probably a rather modest start. Way back when, you may have been answering your own phone or picking up a ringing line if your secretary or receptionist stepped away from the desk. Never forget those days. Callers today are looking for service. They value accessibility. When you provide it, chances are your own business worth or value will increase.

The art of transferring calls

Anyone answering an office line should be trained to ask specific questions to better direct calls and to avoid bouncing callers from one department to another. When making a transfer, moreover, you should brief the person receiving the call so that the caller does not have to repeat him- or herself. For example,

"Mr. Wright, Mr. Jameson is on line one calling about the Chamber of Commerce golf outing."

When a caller is disconnected

You're in the middle of a phone conversation and suddenly there's dead silence. Whose responsibility is it to re-establish contact? If a company representative is talking to a customer or client, that rep should let his or her fingers do the re-dialing—and fast! If two colleagues are talking together, the person who initiated the call should call back.

Handling irate callers

The person on the phone is hopping mad. How can you abide by the guidelines of your company and still make the caller feel as though he or she has come out on top? The courtesy rule that works today is a simple one. Employ the art of good listening. Here are five good listening steps to help you handle a less-than-enjoyable caller.

➙ Let the person speak without interruption. (Again, pause or count to two after you think the person has finished speaking.)

➙ Paraphrase what the person has told you as a way of letting the caller know you have absorbed the message.

➙ Be sure to use the person's name (last name, please) a few times during the conversation.

"I understand what you're saying, Mrs. Douglas."

➙ Explain what you plan to do and then be sure to follow through. For example, if you've told the caller you need to locate her paperwork and will get back to her within an hour, then be sure you return that call by the promised time—even if you haven't been able to locate her paperwork. In any business situation, but especially in one of this nature, trust is of the utmost importance.

➙ When appropriate, follow up in writing. If you were able to meet the person's needs, summarize what you plan to do in writing. If you have not been able to satisfy the person's request, it's still important that you thank the caller for contacting your organization. Let the person know that you appreciated the input (even if it was a negative critique) and emphasize that you hope to do business with him or her in the future.

Slash the slang

Slang is ultra-casual speech and, therefore, not appropriate in a business setting. Easy as it is to fall into the slang trap when you're using the phone, work to avoid phrases like the following:

◆ *"I'm tied up right now."* Sounds like you're involved in something kinky, doesn't it? Perhaps a more appropriate phrase would be, "I have someone in my office. May I return your call in about a half hour?"

◆ *"Hang on."* Just where do you want the person to hang? If this phrase is part of your business vocabulary, get rid of it now. Substitute something more professional. For example, "May I put you on hold, please?"

◆ *"Bye-bye."* Most of us learned this term from our mothers when we were taught to wave. Instead of this elementary-sounding phrase, substitute a simple "good-bye" or "bye-now." Believe me, you'll score higher.

Voice mail etiquette

Like it or not, automation is here to stay—and many people *don't* like it. Although the practicality of voice mail is generally acknowledged, many would-be customers find this form of communication unfriendly. Here are some suggestions for lightening the caller's burden.

☛ Before recording your message, practice it. The terms you use and your voice inflection are important, as they project a definite image.

☛ Make it easy for callers to leave messages. Request minimum information: name, phone number, message. When necessary, the day and time may be requested.

☛ If you're not at your desk to accept incoming calls, check to see whether your voice mail software can route your calls directly to your receptionist. This person should explain that you are unavailable and welcome the caller to leave a message.

☛ If the caller chooses to leave a message, the receptionist should ask whether he or she would prefer to leave it directly on the person's voice mail system.

☛ Be sure to use your voice mail box in the manner for which it was designed—rather than as a method of screening calls.

Note: One voice mail feature most callers appreciate is the option of dialing 0 at the beginning of the message rather than being forced to listen to the entire menu. This puts them directly in touch with the operator.

When you are the caller. When you are the caller, keep these suggestions in mind:

➼ Before dialing, mentally summarize the reason for your call in a few sentences. By doing so, when you are connected to a voice mail box, you'll be ready to leave a concise message.

➼ Speak slowly. Recognize that writing a message takes longer than saying it.

➼ Leave your telephone number. This saves the other person the time of looking it up. This courtesy is especially appreciated when the person you're calling is returning the call from outside the office and doesn't have your phone number at his fingertips.

Updating the "voice." Have you ever thought of your voice mail box or your answering machine as your personal secretary? Essentially, that's what they are. To use your system to the fullest advantage, the key is to think of it as the intermediary between you and your callers.

Keep this mechanical secretary sounding fresh by updating your messages on a regular basis. For some this may mean daily; for others, weekly. Let callers know when they can expect to hear from you. Not only will they appreciate this courtesy; they'll be more apt to leave messages instead of opting for the hang-up routine.

Car phone finesse

This late twentieth-century technological advance brings with it its own system of courtesies.

➼ When receiving a call on your mobile phone, identify yourself with your first name.

➼ When you have passengers in the car, use your phone sparingly, if at all.

➼ When calling someone else's car phone, identify yourself and ask whether it's a good time to talk.

➼ Remember that the clock is running when someone is using a car phone. Discuss only pressing issues. Save the rest for office calls.

➼ Whenever possible, refrain from putting car-phone users on hold.

Speaker phone savvy

Another late twentieth-century convenience, the speaker phone, can be considered either a friend or foe. Most people absolutely despise being put on one. Perhaps they feel they're not receiving the undivided attention of the person on the other end of the line. They may also wonder who else is listening to the conversation.

↤ Speaker phones are only as effective as the people using them. The important rule in speaker phone etiquette is to ask permission before putting someone on the speaker phone. Also, emphasize that your request will be to the benefit of the person on the other end of the line. For example,

"John, George Smith is in my office. I'd like him to benefit from your feedback. Would you mind if I put you on the speaker phone?"

By extending this courtesy, you'll probably find that the person on the other end of the line is flattered.

Perhaps if more people asked permission, rather than automatically putting callers on the speaker phone, this device would become more widely accepted.

When you're not asked

What should you do when you've been put on a speaker phone without being asked and you're not particularly delighted to be talking to an entire office? As in most situations, honesty is the best policy. I recommend you request the person pick up his phone to take your call. If you don't know the person well and are concerned that your request might be offensive, simply say something like, "I can't hear you very well." In most cases the person will automatically pick up the receiver.

Beepers

"Beep-beep-beep!" There's something about that sound . . .

If you choose to use a beeper, invest in a silent one that vibrates to let you know you have a call. I promise you, those in your midst will be most appreciative.

Controlling Call Waiting

↤ Once again, this technological aid can be the source of frustration and resentment in a business setting. If you have Call Waiting on your business line, keep one principle in mind. Asking someone to hold should be the exception rather than the rule.

If you find that someone is exploiting you by asking to put

you on hold to take another call, be bold and take control. Simply say, "I'm sorry, but I don't have time to hold. If you need to take the call, perhaps you can get back to me when we will not be interrupted."

Note: Did you know that some telephone companies provide the feature of allowing you to block Call Waiting from interrupting your line when you're on it? If you have a touch tone phone, before making your call, dial the star button (*) and two numbers preassigned. If you have a rotary phone, before making your call pick up the receiver and dial four preassigned digits. Check with your telephone company to see whether this service is available in your area.

Public phone protocol

You're at the airport, a hotel, or a restaurant between meetings and you need to place a telephone call, but all the public phones are in use. As you wait your turn, keep the following key rules in mind.

➤─0 Stand within an arm's length of the person on the phone so you're not perceived as eavesdropping.

➤─0 Refrain from staring at the person or continuing to look at your watch as a way of trying to get the caller to hang up.

➤─0 If, on the other hand, *you're* the person placing the call, you need only keep one simple rule in mind: Keep the conversation brief. You're on a public phone!

Commonly Asked Questions About Telephone Etiquette

Q. My secretary has told me that some callers seem offended when they're asked if I have their telephone numbers. Is there a more appropriate phrase to use?

A. Although it may hurt some egos to think that the person being called doesn't have the caller's number, it makes sense to take the number when you take a message.

I recommend your secretary simply say, "Let me get your phone number again, Mr. Jones."

If the caller says, "She has my number," one response might be, "Ms. Smith frequently calls in for her messages from outside the office. I'd be happy to take your number so that it is readily available."

Q. We have voice mail at our company. Would you recom-

mend that my staff leave generic messages for callers
("I'm not at my desk right now") or specific ones ("I'll
be in a meeting this morning and will be back in the office this afternoon. Please leave a message so I can return your call at that time. Thank you.")?

A. Your staff should leave messages that are as specific as
possible. Customers and other callers will appreciate
knowing when they can expect a call back. If your staff
chooses to leave specific messages, encourage them to
update them regularly.

Q. Am I the only one annoyed by the question, "How are
you?" How often is the speaker really sincere in want-
ing an answer to this? Isn't there a better way to begin a
conversation?

A. If "How are you?" strikes you as overused or insincere,
you can warm up your telephone conversation with,
"Do you have a minute?"

Q. As an administrative assistant, I am often asked questions for which I do not have an immediate answer. I
feel incompetent responding, "I don't know." Is there a
more professional way to handle this situation?

A. Sure. Simply answer, "That's a good question. Let me
see if I can find the answer for you."
      Be sure to give your response a positive slant. In-
stead of saying, "I don't think I can have an answer until Wednesday," explain, "I can promise you an answer
by Thursday."

Q. Although I hold my clients in high esteem, I become annoyed when I place a call and they request me to call
them back rather than asking whether they can return
my call. Whose responsibility is it to return a call?

A. When someone cannot take a telephone call, that person is responsible for offering to call back at a specific
time rather than asking the caller to play telephone tag.

Q. I receive numerous telephone calls each week from people who are required to sell their service or product by
phone. Is there an appropriate way to get them to leave

me alone?

A. Rather than ignoring calls from such people, either take a minute to accept their calls or delegate a staff person to take them for you. If you're not interested in the product or service, say so graciously. Keep in mind that you or someone from your organization may be calling on that person someday. You know what they say . . . What goes around comes around.

8.

Business Etiquette in Correspondence

With such high-tech, lightning-fast communications devices as computer modems, fax machines, car phones, and the like, you may ask yourself, "Why write it (on paper) when it's quicker to say it (by phone or via computer screen)?" Because in some ways the old axioms that *Talk is cheap* and *Actions speake louder than words* still apply. When someone goes out of his or her way to extend a kindness, for instance, a verbal thank-you is certainly in order. The way to show you're really grateful, however, is still through the written word. When you send an unexpected correspondence, such as a thank-you note or congratulatory card, your actions display a touch of sincerity. These niceties also demonstrate your business sense, in that you have followed through.

Whether you're composing an informal thanks or a more formal correspondence, there are certain written conventions that will give your words the polish that says *class*.

Word wisdom

As you've probably heard from every English teacher you ever had, the opening sentence of your correspondence is all-important. It captures your reader's attention (or it should) and sets the tone for the rest of the communication. That's why it's important to be word-wise from the beginning. The way to do this is to follow rule one for business correspondence: Use a form of thanks in the first sentence.

"Thank you for your interest in our company's product."

"It was a pleasure meeting with you today."

This not only sets a congenial and gracious tone, it gives the impression that you're putting your reader, not yourself, first. This leads us to rule two: Avoid "I."

Many people are tempted to open their notes, letters, and correspondence with this dreaded pronoun. Don't. Using "I" in your first sentence may give the impression that you're putting yourself first.

When is a thank-you note called for?

As a general rule of thumb, a written thank-you note should be sent any time it takes someone more than fifteen minutes to do something for you. Let's say, for instance, that your potential customer schedules time to meet with you. Toward the end of the meeting you thank the person for taking the time to get together. Is a follow-up thank-you letter in order? Yes. It will do three things: confirm your gratitude to your customer or client-to-be, show that you're a person who follows through, and assist you in outclassing your competition.

If you're like most busy people, you might be asking yourself, "Who has time to write all these letters?"

YOU do!

We all make time for things we feel are important. This little extra will help put you in the class to which you aspire—that of a true professional.

Don't procrastinate

▬ Now that I've convinced you (I hope) of the importance of thank-you notes and letters, the obvious question that comes to mind is, "How quickly should they be sent?" While the word "promptly" has many definitions, when it comes to sending thank-you notes and other forms of business correspondence, it has just one meaning—twenty-four to forty-eight hours from the time you communicated with the person. This rule applies to even the busiest people. The closer to the meeting or telephone call a thank-you is sent, the more impact your correspondence will have.

To write or type?

That is the question!

Letters of thanks may be penned when you're sending a note to someone for a courtesy that was extended to you "from one person to another." Thank-you letters may also be handwritten when sending a congratulatory letter, note of condolence, or the like. If, however, you're sending a letter that's likely to be saved or forwarded to someone, I recommend you type it. If you want to add a personal touch, jot a sentence or two on a "stick-um" and attach it to the correspondence. Just make sure it's legible. (One of the hazards of our computer-literate society is that, in many cases, our handwriting makes us look as if we should have been doctors.)

"Marketing" your correspondence

Would you like to develop a writing style that actually makes people look forward to receiving your correspondences?

Impossible, you say? Not really.

By applying a few simple techniques, investing a little extra effort, and polishing your product, you'll crank out notes and letters that will give you that competitive edge. Here are some tips.

Proofread your letters. Even one misspelled word undercuts the effectiveness of your letter. The only way to be assured that your correspondence is error-free is to proofread carefully. If possible, in fact, have a second person proof your document before you send it. Often we "see" on the paper what our mind thinks it put there. A fresh, objective check is always useful—especially in catching typos. Do not be tempted to rely on spell-check software, either, useful as it is. If you are experienced in word processing, you've already found that such software does not catch certain kinds of errors, like homonyms (*see/sea, their/there*) and missing words. Only the human eye can locate these mistakes. Finally, studies repeatedly show that it's easier to catch a typo from a hard copy than from the computer screen. So make the extra effort to crank out a proof copy.

Verify the spelling of all names, first and last. Do this even if you're sending a correspondence to someone whose name, you're told, is "John Smith."

"Mr. Smith, is that J-o-h-n and S-m-i-t-h?"

Nine times out of ten, the odds will be in your favor. There's always that rare occasion, however, when you encounter a "Jon Smith" or a "Jon Smythe" or a "Jean Smith." When you find that a common name has an uncommon spelling, you'll be glad you made the extra effort.

Moreover, this little half-percent shows that you're a person who pays close attention to detail. It's a courtesy that will be remembered. And it just may give others the impression that they simply can't afford *not* to do business with you.

☛ Keep each sentence to ten to twelve words. Shorter sentences frequently make a stronger point. They also attract and keep your reader's attention. So tighten up your writing.

☛ Keep your letter to one page whenever possible. Whether it's a cover letter for a proposal or resume, or a correspondence introducing a new product or service, this guideline should be followed.

One way to accomplish this is to view your letter as having a threefold purpose. The opening paragraph should establish a rapport or reacquaintance with the reader. ("It was a pleasure talking with you yesterday concerning our company's . . .") The middle paragraph should state the purpose of your letter. ("Enclosed is a catalogue, as promised . . .") The closing paragraph should state the next step. ("After reviewing the enclosed proposal, please contact me with any questions . . .")

Twenty-first-century greetings

As we approach the twenty-first century, we're constantly being reminded of how "the rules" change. Nowhere is this more evident than in business communications. Unless you've been living in a time warp, you know that the letters and memos generated in today's offices no longer begin with the long-time generic greeting, "Gentleman:". So how *do* you construct that vital salutation? With care and finesse, of course! Following is some information to help you achieve that goal.

Writing to someone you don't know. When sending a letter to someone you don't know, the rule of thumb is to take the time to learn the name of the person who will be receiving it. If, for example, you're writing to the Human Resources Director of a particular company and you don't know his or her name, take time to phone the company and inquire. While it is perfectly acceptable to write, "Dear Human Resources Director," or simply, "Dear Director," addressing the person by name personalizes the correspondence and certainly adds a desirable dimension.

Patrick or Patricia? Here's one for you. What if you're writing to a "Pat Smith" and the address is a P.O. Box. You have no idea of the company name. What would be the appropriate salutation? In a rare case like this, about the only thing you can do is use the greeting, "Dear Pat Smith:"

If you're an administrative assistant for someone with one of those names that can be either masculine or feminine (Jean/Gene, Joe/Jo, etc.), learn how to let someone know tactfully whether your supervisor is a man or woman. For example,

Caller: *"This is Paul Jenkins from West Side Savings. May I speak with Jean/Gene Cummings?"*

Assistant: *"Certainly. I'll tell Mr. Cummings who's calling."*

If you're trying to determine the sex of the person with whom you wish to speak or correspond, phrase the question diplomatically. For example,

Caller: *"This is Paul Jenkins from West Side Savings. I'd like to send our new brochure to Jean/Gene Cummings and am calling to verify the correct spelling of that name. Can you help me with that?"*

Assistant: *"Certainly. Miss Cummings spells her name J-e-a-n, middle initial A., C-u-m-m-i-n-g-s. Is there any other information you need?"*

"Mrs." Here's a common correspondence mistake. When sending a correspondence to a married woman who has made it known she prefers to be addressed as "Mrs.," many people nowadays have begun using the woman's first name: "Mrs. Mary Smith." Actually, despite all the changes in business etiquette and social protocol, this is not considered correct. The husband's name should still be used: Mrs. John Smith." When a spouse's name is unknown, I recommend that both heading of the letter and the envelope simply read "Mary Smith."

To whom??? When every effort to learn the name of the person with whom you will correspond has met with defeat, address the correspondence, "To Whom It May Concern:". While the intention of the frequently used salutation, "Dear Sir/Madam:" is clear, it should *not* be used. After all, when was the last time you heard a business woman called "Madam"?

First or last? Even with the casualness that has entered many areas of the work place, the more formal use of a person's first and last names is still warranted in many instances. Last names, for example, should be used when

- You are writing to a person you have not met face to face.
- You are writing to a person who has not invited you to use his or her first name.
- The person with whom you are corresponding is matter-of-fact or formal in his or her approach with you.
- You are unsure whether to use the person's last name or first name in the greeting.

If still in doubt, remember . . . rarely can you get in trouble being too formal; but sometimes you can rub a person the wrong way by being too informal.

Signing off

What's an appropriate signature? First name? Last name? Both?

Take your cue from your salutation. If you've addressed the person by first name only, then sign only your first name. If you've used a "Mr.," "Ms.," or other title followed by the last name, then sign both your first and last names ("Sandra Henderson"). In any event, both your first and last name should be typed under your signature.

Promptness pays

I learned this through experience. Let's take a short break from the rules and regulations and protocol so I can share one of my favorite stories.

A few years ago, one of our company's former clients called and explained that her company was soliciting proposals for a Telephone Courtesy workshop. She asked whether our company would like to prepare a proposal.

"Of course!" I said.

My client made a point of telling me that nine other companies had also been invited to bid for this particular project. Without acting phased by her comment, I asked, "When would you like the proposal?"

"A week from Thursday," she responded.

I said, "You'll have it a week from Wednesday."

A week from Wednesday, the proposal—which had been

prepared, proofed, and proofed again—was in her hands. One week later I followed up with my former client to ask whether she and her committee needed anything else from our firm as they were making their decision. She said the proposal was sufficient and that they were still receiving proposals from other companies.

Two months passed. With each telephone call I learned that the number of proposals had been narrowed from ten to eight, then to five, then to three, then to two. Our firm's proposal was still in the running. Better than that, I soon learned that we had been issued the contract. But why?

After the big day of presenting the workshop, my client and I went to dinner. I felt compelled to ask the $64,000 question. "What made our firm's proposal stand out above the rest? Why was it selected from a field of ten?" The answer, I learned, was simple. My client explained that while the other companies prepared excellent proposals, when it came to making the final decision, the committee looked at the total picture. The determining factor that set our proposal apart from those of our competition was that we were the only company to turn in our proposal on time!

What does this story prove? That you don't have to be the smartest or the best to earn business. The key to success is follow-up and follow-through.

Big correspondence mistakes: A review

Why do I continually emphasize punctuality?

For many reasons. Your ability (or inability) to be punctual is a reflection of the kind of person you are. No one wants to conduct business with someone who makes a habit of being late or of not following up within an established time frame.

I also emphasize punctuality in this chapter because, believe it or not, lack of punctuality is one of the most commonly made mistakes of written correspondence. The others, again, are:

- ◆ Using first names when not appropriate

- ◆ Using "Dear Sir/Madam:" in a salutation instead of "To Whom It May Concern:"

- ◆ Using the word "I" in the first sentence of a letter

- ◆ Presenting written correspondence in a sloppy manner—with misspellings, "white out" corrections, grammatical errors, typos, etc.

◆ Failing to make the envelope as professional in appearance as the letter itself

◆ Failing to hold the cover letter to one page

Learn to avoid these blunders and you'll already be ahead in your professional correspondence.

Fax finesse

Who could have envisioned, just a generation ago, that facsimile machines would soon become as common in the work place as an office copier? While this new technology can expedite the transmission of information, it can also sour your relationship with others as quickly as you can send a fax! Here are some tips to help ensure that your fax communication is working for, not against, you and your business.

➤ Send your faxes when promised.

➤ Give your faxes the same professional treatment you do your regular mail. The speed of the technology doesn't give you a license to be sloppy.

➤ For the convenience of the receiving party, always include a cover sheet stating your name, telephone number, fax number, and any other pertinent information.

➤ If you've used correction fluid on your document, be sure to fax a photocopy rather than the original. Correction fluid appears as a blotch when faxed.

➤ Make a photocopy of any document on colored paper. Color slows down the fax transmission, making the procedure costlier and more time-consuming.

➤ Keep the receipt of each fax transmission.

➤ Notify the recipient by phone that the fax has been sent. In large businesses and corporations, a transmission can easily get lost, mistakenly clipped to a previous fax, or routed to the wrong person or department. The intended recipient may finally get the fax hours later or not at all. In either case, your credibility suffers.

➤ Be sensitive about sending more than three or four pages via fax unless you've been requested to do so. When several different faxes are being sent on the same transmission line, or when a fax line is also the person's or company's telephone line, this consideration is appreciated.

Memo manners

Many people never make it past the third rung of the slippery ladder of success. Why? In many cases, because, though they may have polished their image, they have never gotten around to doing the same with their internal correspondences—memos, in particular.

For starters, this form of internal correspondence should be used sparingly. If you send too many memos, your colleagues and staff will begin to think one of two things. You have stock in some paper company. Or you don't have enough to do. The purpose of a memo is to communicate the same information to several persons or to document factual information (company updates, policies, procedures, job descriptions, etc.). If your memo doesn't fit these criteria, don't send it.

Ironically, studies have shown that it takes most managers almost an hour to prepare an average memo. For a $35,000-a-year employee, this means one memo can cost the company $15.75. To help speed up the process and to create efficient, professional-looking memos, consider the following suggestions.

➥ Give your memos the same attention you give the correspondence you send your clients and customers. That means proofread. And then proofread again!

➥ Make your memos efficiency tools. When, for instance, you're requesting a short response to your memos, designate a space on the document. By doing so, you'll save the recipient the added time of creating another document. There's also a good chance you'll hear from the person more promptly.

➥ When sending a memo to people on the same professional level, list their names in alphabetical order.

➥ When sending a memo to people on various professional levels, list them by rank.

Eliminating sloppy correspondence

What if you have your act together about memos and other correspondences, but you unfortunately can't say the same for some of your colleagues? One tactful way to bring sloppy internal documents to the attention of a staff person is to circle the mistake(s) and return a copy to the person who prepared it in the form of a "F.Y.I." If mistakes and sloppiness recur repeatedly, perhaps the situation should be brought to the attention of the person's supervisor. The supervisor, in turn, may suggest that the person attend a business writing course.

To help insure high-quality correspondence from your staff, you might prepare a series of letter formats and encourage staff members to use them. You could also consider putting a rule into effect that any company correspondence that leaves the premises is to be proofed by two people. In this way, typos and grammatical errors may be kept to a minimum.

When to use reply envelopes

Etiquette dictates that any time someone is sent a correspondence and is asked to respond in writing, a business-reply metered or stamped envelope should be included. Besides being appropriate, this consideration displays a definite touch of class.

Proposals with pizzazz

Everyone wants to produce proposals that stand apart from the rest—that is, in a positive way. The substance of a proposal is crucial, of course, but the form and the manner in which it's presented can also make a real difference in how the proposal is viewed by potential customers and clients. Here are five ways to add a touch of style and class to your proposals.

➤—0 Do your homework. Tailor your proposal to the specific interests and needs of your customer or client. Personalizing your document will give it a competitive edge. And it will be obvious that you consider this project important enough to have done research on your own. In many cases, the customer or client will be impressed by your initiative and extra effort.

➤—0 Prepare a professional and polished cover letter. Remember, people buy from people first and companies second.

➤—0 If you receive a telephone call from this potential customer or client, be sure to follow up as soon as possible. (A company I know received an $11 million account. The reason it was selected? It was the only company bidding the project that was courteous enough to return its potential customer's calls promptly!)

➤—0 Once you learn of the decision, send a thank-you letter. If your company won the bid, express your gratitude. If your company was not selected, express your appreciation for having been considered in writing. This correspondence will demonstrate your attention to detail and the touch of class that you will bring (or could have brought) to the table. Remember, there's always a next time.

Commonly Asked Questions About Business Correspondence

Q. Is there an etiquette regarding copies of business letters and memos?

A. Here are a few recommendations.

◆ A copy of the correspondence should be sent to those directly affected by or responsible for the content of the correspondence.

◆ Although "blind copies" (with no names listed) serve the same purpose as an F.Y.I. (For Your Information), they can give the impression that you're doing something behind someone's back.

◆ List names based on pecking order. If all the names listed are on the same order, list them alphabetically.

Q. When addressing correspondence to an official and spouse (i.e., a judge, doctor, etc.), how should the envelope be addressed?

A. If the judge is a man, the envelope should read, "Judge and Mrs. Walter Huber." If the judge is a woman, the envelope should read, "Judge Ann Smith and Mr. Walter Smith."

Q. My coworker and I are having a friendly debate regarding how a folded business letter should be placed in an envelope. Should the unfolded one-third be placed facing the bottom of the envelope or the top?

A. The unfolded one-third faces up. This way, when the envelope is opened with a letter opener, the recipient is not as likely to slit the letter in two.

Q. I recently applied for a position at a well-respected company. At the end of the interview I was told I would be notified—if selected. Although I didn't say anything at the time, my immediate thought was that this organization was missing a goodwill opportunity. In my opinion, any candidate applying for a job should be thanked. Do you agree?

A. Yes. All job candidates should be notified of their selection status. To say nothing is the easy way out. When a company follows through, it not only demonstrates good will, it makes a great public relations gesture that can pay off in the long run.

Q. What is a tactful way to ask clients to pay their overdue bills?

A. When sending a notice for overdue payment, begin by thanking the person or company for past business. Note your company's payment terms and state the problem.

Be sure to give your client or company the benefit of the doubt. For example: "If this bill has been paid within the last ten days, please ignore this reminder." Or, "Since you may not realize that this bill remains unpaid, we would like this letter to serve as a reminder."

Close the letter by thanking your client or customer ahead of time for prompt action.

Note: When designing a collection letter, be sure it complies with the Guides Against Debt-Collection Deception issued by the Federal Trade commission.

Q. A few weeks ago I received a telephone call from a company requesting a bid on a project. After sending it promptly, I followed up and learned that our bid came in too high. The business went to someone else. Do you have any courtesy tips for keeping this relationship alive?

A. Send a letter to the potential client thanking him or her for giving your firm the opportunity to bid on the project. Let the client know that you hope to be asked to bid on upcoming projects. Your follow-through can pay off in only positive ways.

Q. One of our suppliers is going out of business. Is it appropriate to acknowledge this situation?

A. It's definitely in order for you to send a note thanking the company for being your supplier in the past and wishing them well in the future.

9.

The Art of Mingling

Today more than ever before, business relationships are developed and strengthened in social settings. These associations take place over meals, during receptions, at open houses—even on golf courses. It's evident, then, that an understanding of the art of guesting and hosting are important to making the most of these professional/social situations.

As you move through this chapter on mingling, you may wonder why the subject of dining is not included. Because of the importance of this very popular topic, it is treated separately in chapter 10.

For now, let's begin at the beginning—with the invitation.

Invitation etiquette

Whether you are the host/hostess or guest, protocol dictates that you observe the following courtesies.

When you're the host or hostess:

    ☛ Send invitations four to six weeks prior to the scheduled event.

    ☛ Make it easy for guests to respond to the invitations. Include a reply card with a stamped envelope. (As an even greater courtesy, self-address the reply envelope.) Or if you prefer, list a telephone number on the invitation so that guests may call in their replies.

    In either case, be sure to request a date by which you would like your guests to reply. If a get-together is less formal in nature (for example, an open house rather than a sit-down dinner), you may also use "R.S.V.P. Regrets Only."

When you're the guest:

━ Reply to the invitation as soon as possible.

━ If you're not able to attend, offer a brief reason. When you must decline an invitation, try to do so personally by either calling or writing. Don't delegate this task to someone else.

How to overcome *minglephobia*

Being at ease at a social gathering is difficult for many people. Even the most professional and savvy person can suffer from minglephobia. For many, the mere thought of hosting an event or attending a function where image and the ability to schmooz are important can bring on a racing heart and sweaty palms.

Studies show that more than 40 percent of all adults suffer from some sort of social anxiety; in one survey 75 percent said they feel nervous when facing a group of strangers.

If you're one of these people, calm down. You can avoid the disturbing symptoms of minglephobia with a little preventative medicine.

━ Before attending a business/social function, create your own itinerary. In other words, think of people who may be there and make a point of talking to them. You may even want to make a mental list of information about them (recent events in their lives, etc.) to use as ice breakers. By going to an open house or reception with a purpose, you will find it easier to enter a room full of people you don't know extremely well.

━ Read body language. A person standing alone may welcome your company. Groups of three or more may also be approachable. But beware of the twosomes. Study their body language. The old saying about "two's company, three's a crowd" sometimes still applies.

━ If you don't know anyone at the get-together, be honest about it and take the initiative. For example, when approaching a group of people whose body language appears to be open to having others join them, say, "I don't know a soul here, so I thought I'd introduce myself. My name is . . ." Most people can remember being in your shoes and will make you feel welcome and comfortable—at least for a few minutes.

━ Establish instant rapport (see chapter 6, Business Conversation). When you're making small talk, be sure to be sincerely interested in the questions you're asking. If the person with whom you're conversing represents an industry totally unfamiliar to you, try asking a general question like, "How's business?" Inevitably the person will say something that will prompt further conversation.

➥ After mingling for a while, give yourself an "intermission" by talking with people you know. A good rule of thumb to keep in mind is to stay in a group no longer than ten minutes before moving on. This gives you enough time to get involved in small talk without overextending your welcome.

➥ Exit the group tactfully by excusing yourself immediately after you have spoken rather than after someone else has finished speaking.

➥ Take note of the time before going back to the field of unknowns. Decide how long you will continue to work the room before you give yourself another "intermission" or leave the gathering.

➥ Unless you're part of the clean-up committee, don't be one of the last to leave. Wouldn't you rather have others be sorry to see you leave than sorry to see you overextend your stay?

The art of being a good guest
Threats of minglephobia aside, there are certain social niceties that identify you as a good guest.

➥ Arrive promptly.

➥ If you have been invited to bring your spouse, colleague, or "significant other," be sure to brief him or her about others who will be there so that he or she can mingle.

➥ If name tags are not available and someone whose name slips your mind approaches you, simply reintroduce yourself by saying your name and initiating a handshake. In doing so, the other person will probably do the same.

➥ Mingle with people you don't know as well as with those you do.

Now that we've talked about being a good guest, let's take a look at specific business and social situations.

Reception etiquette
The conventions to be followed at a reception depend on what kind of reception it is and on your role at the particular function. When you're the host or hostess, for instance, consider the following.

➥ If fewer than fifty guests will be in attendance, no receiving line is necessary. Instead, you or your co-host should be posted near the door to welcome guests as they arrive.

➡ To help guests become acquainted with one another, supply name tags and thick markers. If possible, try to have the name tags prepared before your guests arrive. A great way to assist guests in meeting one another is to have their first names printed larger than usual.

➡ Greet each guest and talk with the person for a few minutes. Try to introduce each guest to at least one other person. Do not allow your time to be monopolized by getting involved in a lengthy conversation.

➡ Avoid the common gaffe of spending too much time in the kitchen. When planning a gathering in a home environment, arrange to have a catering service handle the details. If this is impractical, arrange for food that can be prepared ahead of time and served without fuss. You want to be able to mingle with your guests, and they should have the opportunity to enjoy your company.

Receptions with no host
This is the kind of gathering generally arranged before a planned event such as a sit-down luncheon or dinner. Although it's the responsibility of each guest to mingle, the organizers of this kind of function are expected to "work the room" and see to it that guests are meeting one another.

Receiving-line manners
Receiving lines are generally in order when fifty or more guests are expected. They are a practical way for guests to have the opportunity to speak with the host or hostess—if only for a brief moment.

If you are to have a receiving line at your function, remember the following:

➡ To avoid congestion, stage your receiving line away from a room's entrance.

➡ The only spouses who should stand in the receiving line are those of the guest of honor and host or hostess.

➡ The host or hostess should refrain from drinking while standing in the receiving line.

➡ A receiving line should last just long enough to give guests a chance to shake hands with the host or hostess and guest of honor.

Buffet etiquette
➤—0 Don't view the buffet table as your last supper! Rather, place on your plate the portion size that you would be presented were you being served.

➤—0 Return for seconds only if you have been invited by your host or hostess to do so.

Banquet etiquette
➤—0 Make a point of talking with a few people at your table, not just the people on either side.

➤—0 Try to include others in the conversation.

Toasting tips
The first toast should be initiated by the host or hostess after guests have been served champagne, wine, or a non-alcoholic beverage. Following are some standard toasting techniques.

➤—0 If the host or hostess has not proposed a toast, it's acceptable for a guest to ask whether he or she may make one.

➤—0 If the setting is formal, the person initiating the toast should stand at his or her seat when proposing it. In less formal settings, the person may remain seated if desired.

➤—0 Toasts should be brief.

➤—0 When you are a guest, after the person being honored has been toasted, raise your glass and, looking at the honoree, nod your head in a slight bow before taking the first sip.

➤—0 If you're the person being toasted, do not raise your glass as the toast is being made. Raise it after the toast has been made with a phrase like, "And to good friends!"

Alcoholic beverages
In many of the seminars I've conducted, the question, "How many drinks is too many?" is frequently posed. The answer, of course, varies with the tolerance level of each individual. Your company's guidelines on this matter should also be considered before you order alcoholic beverages. As a standard guideline, however, if you choose to have an alcoholic beverage, be sure you remain in control. Don't let it control you. If you're representing your organization and are even slightly more relaxed after consuming an alcoholic beverage, you've probably already had one too many!

Corporate teas

Some corporations have found that offering corporate teas sets them apart from the competition. There's no doubt that such a function helps establish an image of class and polish. This kind of get-together, which is typically the last scheduled meeting of the day, is held in a hotel salon or living room setting; needless to say, tea is the beverage of the hour.

Custom dictates that guests be served in one of two ways. According to the first way, each serves his or her own tea and helps himself or herself to the accompanying finger sandwiches, desserts, etc. Each person then takes a seat at the table, on the couch, etc.

The alternative calls for guests to be served their tea while seated at tables. Finger sandwiches, cookies, petit fours, chocolates, etc., are set out on trays at each table. In either case, sterling silver utensils and cloth napkins should be used.

Golfcourse proprieTEES

If you think finessing is reserved for the bridge table, you've probably never been on a golf course. But chances are, you will. Golf outings have become one of the most popular forms of corporate entertaining and socializing. Following are a few basic rules of golf etiquette.

➤ Always be ready to play when it's your turn.

➤ Guests are usually invited to tee off first (rank also prevails).

➤ The golfer furthest from the green always plays first.

➤ When someone is addressing the ball, stand still and refrain from talking.

➤ Help others enjoy the game by offering compliments like, "Nice shot" or "Good swing."

➤ Safety as much as courtesy dictates that you remain in control of your emotions and refrain from immature actions like throwing your club.

➤ When walking with a hand cart, never pull it across the tee or the green.

➤ When using a riding cart, be sure to understand and follow the course rules. Examples: Carts must remain on paths at all times. Carts may cross fairways at 90 degrees. Always keep carts at least fifteen yards from the green.

➤ When putting, do not step in your playing partner's

putting line. (Impressions left on the grass can affect the roll of the ball.)

    ➶ Be a good sport.

When it comes to building healthy and lasting business and social relationships, your behavior on the golf course is much more important than your score.

The art of gift giving

Invariably, in discussions of business/social functions, the question of gifts is raised. Customs and protocol vary from company to company regarding such issues as birthday and wedding gifts, sympathy acknowledgments, etc., but some basic gift-giving guides apply across the board.

Whenever you're invited to someone's home for dinner, for instance, or even for an open house, taking a small gift is in order. Depending on the tastes of the recipient, the gift should be a box of candy, a potted plant, a bottle of wine—something simple.

When you're on the receiving end, custom dictates certain behavior. Whether the gift is food, wine, or an enticingly gift-wrapped mystery package, it should be opened after the guests have left. This will spare an embarrassing moment for any guests who did not display their thoughtfulness in this way.

What about thank-you notes? Does a verbal thank-you suffice? No. Remember the guideline explained in chapter 8. If it takes someone longer than fifteen minutes to do something nice for you, a written thank-you is definitely in order.

Commonly Asked Questions About Business Entertaining

Q. Please discuss appetizer etiquette. I have attended many after-hours business functions and am appalled at some of the uncouth manners displayed there. Guests will dip already-bitten tortilla chips into salsa, leaving it unpalatable for others. Others will fill their plates as though they are there for dinner rather than hors d'oeuvres. Please let people know that when they are invited to open houses and receptions, they are there to socialize first and eat second.

A. Appetizer etiquette dictates that the dip be placed on and eaten from one plate rather than from the serving bowl. Portions should be small.

Q. Please let people know that it is gauche to drink beer
from a bottle when they are in a reception environment.
Recently we invited one of our associates to a reception
honoring one of our clients. He ordered beer from the
open bar without requesting a glass. I was very embarrassed. I wanted to say something but didn't, for fear of
damaging his ego. Is there a way I could have tactfully
made the point that drinking beer and using a glass go
hand-in-hand at business gatherings?

A. I am in complete agreement with you. In the situation
described, a glass should have been requested.

Q. When attending after-hours business functions, when is
it appropriate to offer my business card to someone I've
just met?

A. I recommend you offer your card to a "stranger" if it
sounds as though the person might want it. If, for instance, he or she has expressed an interest in your company's products or services, then by all means offer
your business card.

Q. I am planning a black tie function for our company.
Dinner will be served at this event. When arranging the
place cards on the tables, should I seat each woman to
the left or the right of her spouse or guest?

A. To the left. To remember this rule of social etiquette, re-
call the tradition from which it sprang: A woman is always seated closest to the heart of her spouse or guest.

Q. Our company has a few get-togethers each year.
Spouses are always invited. During the past six months
I have divorced and do not know whether it would be
better to ask one of the "significant others" I am dating
to an upcoming dinner or to attend alone. My invitation
said, "and guest."

A. While inviting a guest may be more comfortable, be
sure to invite someone who presents him- or herself in
the manner in which you wish to be represented. If the
current "significant other" cannot meet your criteria of
polish, charm, personality, etc., then go alone—and
have fun!

10.

The Mechanics of Table Manners and Restaurant Etiquette

Most people invite others to lunch in order to develop or maintain business or personal relationships. In these social situations, your table manners say a lot about you and the way you conduct business. They demonstrate the attention to detail that should be an integral part of the philosophy of any employee who wants to achieve and maintain a competitive edge. Perhaps that's why so many second and third job interviews are scheduled around meals.

A word of warning. As you get into this chapter, you'll notice it's by far the longest one in the book. There's a lot to cover. When presented at seminars, this topic of dining out is always the one that sparks the most interest and elicits the most questions. It's also the most fun. So get ready to put your best fork forward!

Dining decorum

To enjoy the image of a polished professional who knows his or her restaurant manners, remember the five rules of business dining.

→ When meeting someone in a restaurant, wait in the lobby unless otherwise requested.

→ If you're the first to be seated, wait until everyone has arrived before ordering a beverage.

→ Determine the appropriate price range by asking your host, "What do you recommend?" Do not simply order the stuffed lobster.

━0 Order only the basics (salad, main course, and beverage). If your host suggests an appetizer or dessert, be guided accordingly.

━0 Maintain the same pace of eating as the person with whom you are dining. If the person is a slow eater, expand on a mutually interesting topic while he or she is eating. If you're a slow eater, ask the person a question that might take a few minutes to answer—such as, "What's the most gratifying part of your job?"

Seating with style

Now attend while I unlock the mysteries of seating protocol.

If you and your spouse are hosting guests, here's the appropriate way to seat them. If you are a man, the most important female should be seated to your immediate right. The second-most important female should be seated to your immediate left. The most important male should be seated to your spouse's immediate right, and the second-most important male should be seated to your spouse's immediate left (see diagram).

When you are the host or hostess of a single guest, your guest should be seated to your immediate right. One reason for

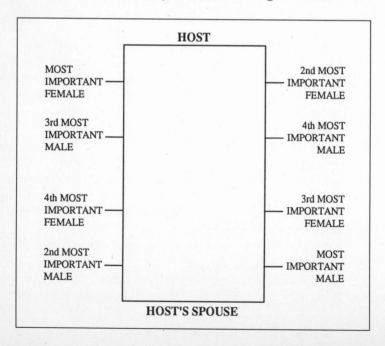

this is that "serving etiquette" dictates that meal orders be taken from the guest first (who should be seated to the right of the host or hostess). If the guest to the right of the host or hostess is a man and the person to his right is a woman, the first order typically taken by a server is from the woman (see diagram on page 94).

Note: Seating protocol during meals varies from country to country. If you're planning a business trip abroad, refer to the list of suggested readings at the end of this book for detailed information.

Napkin placement

➡ "When should I place my napkin on my lap?" is a question that invariably comes up at my seminars and workshops. Custom and decorum dictate that you place the napkin on your lap as soon as everyone has been seated. Etiquette also dictates that guests wait for the host or hostess to do so before following suit.

➡ When the napkin is displayed in a goblet, it's usually best to wait for the server to present it to you. This is frequently the protocol in French restaurants. If you're unsure of what to do, simply take the cue from your host or hostess.

When you do place your napkin, don't come off as some kind of magician, shaking it over the table as if you're trying to make a rabbit appear. Simply open it as you place it on your lap. And be sure to keep your napkin folded in half with the crease toward you.

➡ At the close of the meal, make sure your napkin stays on your lap until everyone at the table has finished eating and drinking. At that point, napkins should be placed to the right of the place setting. Note: These napkin norms also apply to the paper variety. A napkin should never be wadded and left on the table.

Getting your server's attention

➡ When hosting or hostessing a meal, think of the server as one of your employees. In other words, treat him or her with respect. When you have a request, for instance, wait until your server is serving you and then ask, "When you return, will you bring some extra butter, please?" By displaying this courtesy, you will demonstrate both to the server and to those in your midst that you respect the time of others. Almost as important, you'll probably get better service!

If the service is poor and your server is not within sight, try making eye contact with another server. If you're the host or hostess and all else fails, excuse yourself from the table and find the manager on duty. Whatever you do, avoid "hailing" a server. You can be assured that most restaurant staff members despise this gesture—especially when more than one guest is trying to get his or her attention in this way.

Gushing with gratitude

How many times should a server be thanked during a meal?

My recommendation is, each time you are served. Forms of thanks include a verbal thank-you, a smile, or even a nod. The only time it may be inappropriate to thank a server is when someone is talking with you and you prefer to not break eye contact.

Territorial techniques

You have been seated and your napkin has been placed on your lap. You have placed your order. The person next to you is offering you the basket of rolls. Did you ever wonder which bread plate was yours? It's one of those moments of hesitation, isn't it?

So that you'll never have to be concerned about such awkward interludes again, remember these important table manner tips.

☛ Solids to your left; liquids to your right. You may already know this rule. But what if the person seated to your left doesn't realize that or he or she just placed his or her roll on your bread and butter plate? There are several ways to handle this potentially embarrassing situation. The first is to thank the person for the roll and begin eating it. (You can bet the etiquette offender will not use your bread plate again!) Another solution is simply to use the bread and butter plate to your right, thus causing everyone at the table to use the wrong plates.

If you're brave, you can wait for the server to return and ask, "May I have another bread and butter plate?" (Be sure to say it just loudly enough so that the person on your left gets the point.) Or, finally, you can forego having a roll and philosophize that, after all, this isn't your last supper!

Note: A common gaffe made by left-handers is to reach for the beverage glass with the left hand rather than with the right, drink from it, and set it down on the left side of the place setting rather than back on the right. Watch out, lefties!

☛ Pick up your utensils from the outside in. When you're

unsure of which utensil to use, simply begin by using the utensils on the outside and working your way in toward the plate. For example, the salad fork is always placed on the left side, farthest away from the plate—if your place has been properly set, that is.

Note: If you're partaking in a prearranged meal, the spoon or fork above the place setting should be used for dessert.

➤─0 Offer community food to others before helping yourself. If the rolls, sugar, sweetener, salt and pepper, cream, etc. are closest to you, before helping yourself, offer the items to the person on your left. This rule applies only to the person who is starting the food and condiments around the table.

➤─0 Pass food to the right. Food should be passed counterclockwise. This procedure also supports the seating etiquette rule that your guest be seated to your right.

If you're dining with colleagues and you're beginning to pass the community food, you may offer it to the person to your left, help yourself, and then proceed to pass it to your right.

➤─0 Allow food that has been preordered to be served to you, even if you know you won't like it. Let's say you're attending a banquet and can see from what's being served to the other guests that you are not going to like the soup. What to do?

Even if you know you abhor sweet potato soup, I suggest you allow it to be served to you. By doing so, you will ensure that those around you feel comfortable as they begin the course. By refusing the soup—or any other course, for that matter—you may make others feel hesitant about beginning the meal. As a way of looking as though you are participating in the soup course, lay your spoon in the soup bowl or on the service plate. Keep your utensils in one of these positions, and those around you may be more at ease to enjoy their soup.

What's your style?
Depending on how you've been raised, you participate in meals in one of three ways—the American style of dining, the European (or Continental) style of dining, or the NO style of dining.

Dining American-style.
Step One. When cutting a piece of food, place your fork in your left hand with the handle hidden in the palm of your hand and the fork tines down. Place the knife in your right hand with the handle hidden and the serrated edge facing the plate.

Step Two. After cutting one piece of food, lay your knife across the top of your plate with the serrated edge facing you. Transfer the fork from your left hand to your right—with the fork handle now showing between your index finger and thumb and the tines facing up.

Step Three. After chewing and swallowing the piece of food, repeat the first three steps.

Step Four. When you choose to lay your utensils down to rest or to listen more intently to the people with whom you're dining, the "rest" position should place the knife across the top of the plate with the serrated edge toward you. Place your fork, tines up, with its handle resting on the lower right side of the plate (see diagram 1).

Step Five. When you've completed your meal, place your fork across the center of the plate with the handle to the right and the fork tines down. Bring your knife from across the top of the plate and place it next to the fork with the blade still facing you (see diagram 2).

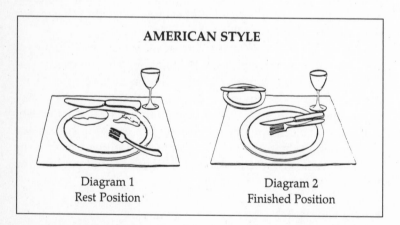

AMERICAN STYLE

Diagram 1
Rest Position

Diagram 2
Finished Position

Dining European-style

Step One. Follow step one of the American style.

Step Two. Rather than transferring the fork to your right hand, leave the knife and fork in the same positions as described in step one. With your knife in your right hand, lift your fork (containing a bite-size piece of food) to your mouth, tines down.

Step Three. When you're ready, repeat the first three steps.

Step Four. In European or Continental style, the "rest" position involves placing your knife on the plate first, with its handle to the lower right of the plate. Next place your fork, tines down, on the lower left of the plate so that fork and knife cross (see diagram 3).

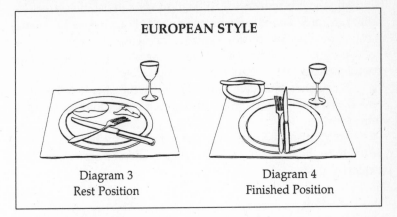

EUROPEAN STYLE

Diagram 3
Rest Position

Diagram 4
Finished Position

Step Five. When you've completed your meal, place your utensils in a 12 o'clock and 6 o'clock position.

Dining with NO style
This variation consists of keeping your knife in your hand while handling your fork like a shovel. The NO style of dining also involves holding your fork with the tines up and handle showing while cutting a piece of food. There's only one thing to say about this style—don't do it!

Beverage etiquette
➤ Let's get it out in the open . . . ice is not the edible part of a beverage. In other words, don't chew ice.

Iced tea. When served a wedge of lemon with a glass of iced tea (or water, as some restaurants do these days), cup your hand in front of the lemon as you are squeezing it into your glass. By doing so, you'll keep the person across from you from getting "lemon fresh."

Coffee. While many people drink coffee morning, noon, and night, when you're dining it should be requested after the main course has been cleared and before dessert is offered. Coffee was made to be consumed as an after-dinner beverage, so treat it accordingly.

Alcoholic beverages. This is always a spirited topic. To simplify matters, most companies today have the following written or unwritten policy: If business is to be discussed after lunch, an alcoholic beverage should not be consumed. For business dinners, most companies and businesses trust their employees to use their good judgment. Of course, whatever the situation business etiquette dictates that you not allow your drink to speak for you.

If you choose to have a mixed drink, remember that the "stirrer" is just that—something with which to stir. Don't use it as a ministraw!

This is also a good place to remind you of the beer by-law referred to in the last chapter. Remember . . . don't be tacky. Always request a glass.

Wine wisdom

Don't let thoughts of menu columns of fancy wine names or prim and proper sommeliers intimidate you. Actually, you don't have to be a wine connoisseur to choose or enjoy a bottle of wine. Simply become acquainted with a few varieties. Even if you're not a wine expert, you can host a meal with savvy. Let's start with ordering.

If wine isn't your expertise, don't risk embarrassing yourself. Rather than pointing to the wine list, mispronouncing a name, taking a wild guess because the name sounds sophisticated, or saying that you'd like to order "number 14," try these alternatives.

➱ Ask the wine steward (sommelier) to tell you and your guests about the house wine(s) and to make a recommendation.

➱ Ask one of your guests who may be familiar with wine to do the honors of ordering for the group.

When you're acting as the host or hostess and ordering wine for your guests, you have three responsibilities. The first is to taste the wine before your guests do. This is to ensure that you're not being served a spoiled or flawed wine. You're not tasting to determine whether you *like* it; the assumption is that when you ordered the wine, you had enough knowledge to know how it should taste and that your choice would be compatible with the meal.

When the bottle is presented by the sommelier—before it's even opened—acknowledge with a nod of the head that the wine you ordered is, indeed, the one being presented (don't forget to check the vintage, or date). After it has been opened for you, check the cork for moistness to be sure it has been properly stored. Once you have given your approval, a small amount will be poured into your glass for you to taste. After tasting and judging it acceptable, give a final nod to the server or sommelier, who will proceed to pour for the first woman to your right—and then for the other guests.

Is there a graceful way to send flawed wine back? Yes. Just do it! If you're presented a bottle of wine with a dry cork, that's an indication that it may have been stored improperly and could be oxidized or spoiled (air has entered the bottle). In such cases, restaurants are happy to replace the bottle. Simply bring the situation to the attention of the wine steward—tactfully, of course.

How often does something like this happen? As restauranteurs tell it, only about 10 percent of the wines returned by patrons are actually bad. It's more common for diners to be unfamiliar with the wine in question or to request a new bottle simply for the sake of impressing their guests. In other words, never send back a bottle of wine unless it is truly flawed. If you've ordered something that doesn't meet your tastes, that's too bad. The solution is simply to order another selection.

Your next responsibility is to be sure that each of your guests has sufficient wine. When ordering, expect to get about eight servings from every bottle and calculate accordingly. The art of being a good host or hostess includes becoming familiar with the patterns of your guests. If, for instance, you know that one of your guests enjoys wine just a tad bit more than perhaps he or she should, schedule a shorter "drinks before dinner" interlude. After the meal, serve only coffee—no after-dinner aperitifs or liqueurs.

See to it that the glasses of your guests are replenished as you're all enjoying the wine. Guests should never have to refill their own wine glasses. In carrying out this responsibility, consider the following.

When serving red wine, fill an eight-ounce glass approximately half way. This allows the bouquet of the wine to expand.

When pouring a glass of white wine, fill it three-quarters of the way. Not as much air is needed to enhance the bouquet of most white wines.

Whether you are the host or hostess or a guest, here is a final word of wine wisdom. When lifting a glass of wine, do so from the stem rather than from the globe or bowl. This prevents your body temperature from warming the wine, if it's white, and allows you to enjoy its clarity, if it is red.

Bread and rolls
Congratulations. You've successfully claimed the left-hand bread plate as your own. But you're not out of the woods yet!

Butter wrappers. At this point in a meal, many experience one of those awful moments of hesitation when they wonder what to do with their butter or margarine wrappers. If you receive the butter or margarine in a relatively soft state, just leave it in the wrapper as you place it on your roll with your knife.

If the pat is hard, remove it from the wrapper with your knife and place it on your plate. Then fold the wrapper in half or in fourths and set it on the side of the bread plate or under its rim.

Bread dos and don'ts. When eating a roll or a slice of bread, tear off a bite-sized piece, butter it, lay the knife across the top of your bread plate (always with the serrated edge toward you) and then enjoy. Be sure to swallow the first piece before picking up your knife again.

A common gaffe when eating rolls is to cut or break the roll in two, butter half, and then begin munching. This is not considered good manners. If you want to come off as someone with class, follow the method already described.

Crumbs. How do you handle those crumbs that invariably land all over your place setting and sometimes even your lap? Is it appropriate to brush them carefully to one side or off the table? Not unless you want a job! Be careful. The restaurant manager might hire you.

When you're dining, do just that—dine! Don't try to assist the hired help.

Mopping up. Another question that often comes up is whether its ever O.K. to use a roll or a piece of bread to sop up that last bit of gravy, sauce, or food. The answer is, certainly—if you happen to be at home with the blinds pulled. *Never* when dining.

The last roll. And finally, what do you do if you'd like another roll and there's only one left in the basket? Should you take it? Again, only if you're viewing this meal as your last supper. A more appropriate response is to wait until your server returns and then request more rolls or bread. As a guest, no matter how much you'd like that last roll, even if it is offered to you, you should refuse. (It's acceptable, of course, to be less formal with family and friends. So bend the rule accordingly.)

Soup-eating tips

Soup is another topic that brings scores of questions from seminar participants. How do you eat the stuff gracefully? Should you spoon away or toward your mouth? What if you accidently slurp? Should you crumble crackers into the bowl? The list goes on and on.

A few years ago I received a telephone call on our etiquette hotline from a woman in Washington, D.C. She was calling with a pressing question about soup. It seems she was dating a high-powered politician, and it really bothered her that he tipped his soup bowl. She wanted to know if it was correct to do so.

My answer was that it's always appropriate to tip a soup bowl—if it contains a handle and if the person really needs that last drop. To carry off this gesture gracefully and appropriately, tip the bowl away from you—the same direction in which the soup spoon should be moved.

With that in mind, remember the following super tips for eating soup.

↝ Unless you're in Japan, where it's perfectly acceptable to lift the cup to your lips and slurp, play it safe by moving the spoon away from you to fill it and then back toward your mouth. This allows any excess to spill into the bowl rather than on you. Also, rather than do a "forward march," delicately sip soup from the side of the spoon. Try to do so with minimal or no sound effects.

↝ If your soup is too hot to eat, the common-sense solution is to wait for it to cool down. Never blow on it, stir it, or drop in an ice cube.

↝ If you want crackers in your soup, wait until you get home. When dining, the only crackers that may legitimately be added to your soup are oyster crackers. Instead, open the package and place the crackers either on your soup service plate or on your bread and butter plate. Enjoy the soup and the crackers, but not simultaneously. *Either* the cracker or the soup spoon should be in your hand at any given moment. It is not appropriate to sport the soup spoon in one hand and a cracker in another while eating them in rotation.

☛ Most people hold onto their utensils for dear life until a course has been completed. (Maybe this is a carry-over from the pre-McManners generation "clean-plate club.") It's perfectly acceptable, however, to lay down the soup spoon every few bites. When resting, the soup spoon should be laid in the soup cup or bowl.

☛ Once you have completed the soup course, place the soup spoon on the right-hand side of the service plate. The server can then remove this course from the right, lifting the service plate, soup cup or bowl, and spoon in one quick movement.

Salad

Can you believe that it takes this much energy to dine? I warned you . . . when it comes to meals, there's a lot to consider. To insure that you are the picture of propriety during the salad course, observe the following suggestions.

☛ Wait for everyone at the table to be served before beginning.

☛ Start passing the salad dressing *only* if you are the person closest to it. When everyone at the table is "equal," the dressing should first be offered to the person to the left of the initiator. Then that person should use it before passing it to the right. When those at the table are not all equals, the dressing should be passed to the host's or hostess's right—that is, to the most important guest present.

☛ Cut your lettuce with your knife, if you wish. These days, you may cut anything that does not walk by itself and is edible. In days gone by it was considered uncouth to cut salad with a knife because silverware was then made of steel, not stainless steel, and the acidity from the salad dressing would tarnish the knife.

Note: The etiquette code of not cutting lettuce still applies in some European countries. See the list of recommended readings for details.

☛ Master difficult-to-eat salad ingredients so they don't control you. Cherry tomatoes, for instance, are notorious for providing moments of hesitation. Is it acceptable to cut a cherry tomato with your knife? That depends on how much you like the person sitting across from you! If you must cut, do so by gently piercing the tomato with your fork first. This releases the pressure and allows you to cut without squirting tomato juice across the table.

🖛 Another potential awkward moment presents itself whenever unpitted olives find their way into the salad. What's a stylish diner to do when confronted with an olive pit in the mouth—one that must either be swallowed or removed in a delicate fashion? Don't get uptight. Just remember this axiom: Whatever goes in with a utensil comes out with a utensil. In the case of an olive pit, a fork or spoon should receive the pit and transport it safely to the edge of the plate. Most people find the spoon provides more balance.

🖛 Give your server the proper cues. Let him or her know when you are "resting," as opposed to finished. As with the soup spoon, it is most appropriate to lay your salad fork down after every few bites rather than holding on to it for dear life until you've completed the course.

To let the server know you're resting, simply place the fork on your plate with the handle on the right, keeping the fork tines up. If you've already used your knife, place it across the top of your plate with the serrated edge facing you (see diagram on page 100).

Note: To review the differences in "rest" position between American and European dining, see page 101.

🖛 To let the server know you've completed the salad course, place your fork on the plate with the handle on the right—this time, with the tines down. After you've placed your fork in the "finished" position, transfer your knife across the top of an available plate (probably your bread plate).

Observing these rules of etiquette will eliminate the situation in which we've all found ourselves at one time or another. Can you identify with this scenario? You have completed your salad and your knife is on your salad plate. As the server prepares to remove your plate, he or she inquires, "Would you like to keep your knife?"

This is a tactful way of saying, "Move your knife."

Anyway, now you know.

Appetizer amenities

🖛 One of the most commonly committed sins at the appetizer buffet is eating directly from the serving plate. To avoid this catastrophe, simply follow this common-sense rule: Place whatever you would like to eat on your plate (and that includes dips and salsas) before indulging.

Main-course manners

Now that you've successfully and stylishly wined and dined your way through two courses, let's move on to the main feast.

➵ As you probably already know, it is most appropriate to wait for everyone at the table to be served before indulging. If you're a guest, play it safe by going one step further and waiting for the host or hostess to take the first bite before digging in yourself. After this ceremonial first bite, you can proceed with the main course, bearing in mind the following suggestions.

➵ Cut (don't "saw") one piece of food at a time. This helps both to moderate the pace of the meal and to preserve the aesthetic quality of the food's presentation as long as possible. (Hey! Who said dining was always fun? Sometimes it's hard work!)

➵ Use *only* the fork and knife during the main course. You're probably couth enough to observe this dining dictum of your own accord, and so would never dream of using your spoon for peas or mashed potatoes, as some do. Of course you wouldn't.

Salad as the main course

Since it's only during the last couple of decades that salad has become a common main-course entree, a commonly asked question is, "Which fork should be used when eating something like a Cobb or Chef Salad as your main course?"

➵ Always use your main-course fork. It's the utensil of choice for handling the chunks of meat, cheese, etc., that are generally included in a healthy salad entree.

Finessing difficult foods

Sometimes business dining can seem more like a battle than a feast. Here are some suggestions for handling those difficult foods.

Spaghetti. Do you cut your spaghetti, or twirl it? If you choose the latter (the European way), then you're doing it right. I suggest that you use a spoon to assist in securing the strands to the fork—in true Italian fashion.

Corn on the cob. Believe it or not, there is a stylish way to eat corn on the cob—typewriter style. It's simple. Butter and salt your corn a few rows at a time and then nibble across. When you get to the end of the row, however, you don't have to "hit the return." Rather, continue to eat from the side where you left off.

Peas and other hyperactive vegetables. As everyone knows, eating foods like peas, corn, and rice can be tricky. When you're faced with any of these foods and are down to the last few nibbles, here's what I recommend.

If you're an honorary member of the "clean plate club" and you're merely *eating,* use your knife to assist these vegetables onto your fork. Before taking the fork to your mouth, however, be sure to lay the knife down, across the top of your plate, with the blade toward you.

If, on the other hand, you are truly *dining,* the following rule applies: If you can't get a particular food onto your fork without the assistance of your knife, you probably don't need it to begin with. In other words, consider the meal *finis!*

Chicken. Even though it may be finger lickin' good, chicken (in a business setting) should always be eaten with utensils. And that about says it all.

Ribs. Based as I am in Cincinnati (considered by the locals to be the rib capital of the world), I'm constantly being asked about the appropriate way to enjoy these spicy wonders. I always respond with the following story, which was shared with me during a seminar.

Two businessmen from a Cincinnati-based company had a customer from New York at their headquarters and decided to take their visitor to dinner at a family restaurant known nationwide for its ribs. Once seated, all three ordered spareribs.

In due time the main course arrived, and the two locals automatically began eating the ribs with their fingers while the New Yorker proceeded to employ his fork and knife. Obviously, the Cincinnatians noticed the eating habits of their guest. But did the New Yorker take note of his hosts' habits?

Well, by and by the New Yorker returned to Cincinnati and was asked by the same two businessmen where he would like to dine. Back they went to the same family restaurant, where all three once again ordered the ribs. This time, however, when the dinners arrived, the two locals made a point of eating the ribs with their utensils. Not the New Yorker. He used—you guessed it—his fingers.

A simple rule applies. When in Rome . . . As a final note, however, when you're unsure what to do—when you experience one of those moments of hesitation—you can hardly ever get into trouble by being too formal.

Ketchup. Now, don't snicker. It *is* possible to be sophisticated and still enjoy ketchup. But my recommendation for smoothly getting a blob out of a bottle that's been sitting around for a while is to hope that someone else uses it first.

When, however, it's up to you, turn the bottle three-quarters of the way upside down. Then insert an unused knife in the bottle to mediate the ketchup's flow. Of course you're left with the obvious dilemma—what to do with that doggone knife. Just place it discreetly on an available plate (an empty one, of course).

Condiments. When you're a guest, you should eat only what's served. If you enjoy ketchup and Worcestershire sauce on your steak and it's not on the table, live without it. If your host or hostess requests it, that's a different story.

Excusing yourself during a meal

If you find it necessary to excuse yourself from the table for a fleeting moment, do so only between courses. In this situation, lay your napkin either on the chair or on the left-hand side of your place setting. By placing it in either of these positions, you'll be providing a cue to the server that you will be returning.

An awkward problem

Many people ask about the suggested diplomatic procedure when the person you're with has something on his or her mouth. It depends. If you're with a friend, it's probably acceptable to say, "You have a speck of something on your mouth. I know I really appreciate it when someone points out something like that to me." In the case of, say, a supervisor or new client, on the other hand, a good tactic is to blot your own mouth. It's human nature for others to mimic this gesture sooner or later. Try it sometime. It's amazing.

Synchronizing your pace

If you're a fast eater, you probably find yourself frequently being the first to finish a meal. If you're a slow eater, you are most likely one of the last to complete your meal, while others are waiting for you to finish.

To eliminate feelings of awkwardness, take note of the eating patterns around you. See if it's fast, slow, or moderate; and then follow suit. Or find a way to complement the pattern of those with whom you're dining.

For example: If you find yourself eating with a fast eater, and you're a slow eater, get the person to talk by asking a few open-ended questions. This may slow down the other person's eating pace and help to speed yours up a little.

The four commandments
Since this chapter has made dining out with clients and colleagues sound like something akin to a religious experience, let's wrap it up with the four dinner commandments.

➛0 Realize the purpose of business dining. Picture this. You're at a restaurant. You've ordered filet mignon and have requested that it be prepared medium well. When it's served, you find it's been prepared medium rare. What should you do?

In this situation you are obliged to recognize the inconvenience you might cause the others at your table by sending the food back. They may, for instance, feel obligated not to begin their meals until yours is returned. By requesting that your food be prepared to your liking rather than accepting it as it is, you will be breaking the momentum of the meal.

Remember, the main purpose of a business meal is to build rapport. Eating comes second. The only time it's acceptable to return food to the kitchen is when a few people find it necessary to send their meals back.

➛0 Be discreet with undesirable food and foreign substances. Let's say that as you're eating you discover a hair on your plate. Whatever you do, be discreet about mentioning it to the server. If you're in the company of others, don't make it part of the conversation. Rather, eat something else (a roll, for instance) until the server returns to your table. Then, in a low voice, request that your meal be replaced. Most servers will pick up on your cue immediately.

➛0 Do not blow your nose at the table. It's "no" to nose blowing while dining. If you feel you absolutely must clear your sinus passages, simply excuse yourself and take care of the matter. "What about coughing?" I'm often asked. "Is it more appropriate to turn your face to the right or to the left?" All I can say to that is that I guess it depends on whom you like least. Seriously, cough if you must; just do it as discreetly and inoffensively as possible—always covering your mouth, of course.

⊶ Provide a taste of your food in an appropriate manner. Just what is the appropriate way to share food? Before beginning the particular course, cut the piece you are sharing with an unused utensil. Offer your plate to the person with whom you're sharing your meal. The person should take the piece being offered and put it on his or her plate with an unused utensil before returning the plate to you.

Commonly Asked Questions About Table Manners and Restaurant Etiquette

Q. When participating in a business meal, is it appropriate to initiate saying grace?

A. If you're entertaining clients in your home, it would be appropriate to initiate a prayer before the meal. When, however, you're being entertained in someone else's home or are dining in public, it would be more appropriate to say a private grace as inconspicuously as possible.

Q. My wife and I need your advice. We are disputing whether it is appropriate for me to protect my tie by covering it with a napkin. What is acceptable?

A. Although covering your tie with a napkin—or worse, flipping it over your shoulder—may save on the dry-cleaning bills, such actions are not considered good etiquette. Sorry!

Q. Is it really appropriate for Americans to eat European style? I once heard that Americans were perceived as pretentious when they chose to eat in this fashion.

A. Americans may choose either tradition. Whatever the choice, consistency should be maintained throughout the meal.

Q. Nothing is more repulsive to me than seeing people eat ice cream by moving it "in and out" of their mouths and taking a bite each time. Please comment.

A. Food that goes into the mouth should never come out again, unless it's inedible (gristle, olive pit, etc.).

Q. What is the correct behavior when, over a business meal, my client orders a martini and I would like an iced tea?

A. You're certainly never obliged to order an alcoholic drink. Whatever you choose, order with confidence. Be sure not to make excuses for ordering the drink of your choice.

Q. Is there a diplomatic way of setting a time limit for business lunches? Sometimes my clients like to linger over meals.

A. The next time you invite a client to lunch, instead of asking, "Would it be convenient?" ask, "Would noon to one-thirty be convenient?" Be sure, however, to choose a restaurant that can provide such timely service.

Q. Recently my boss asked me to schedule a luncheon meeting with a few of our suppliers. We met in a restaurant, and when the check arrived, my boss made no attempt to take care of it. Since I arranged this meeting, should I have taken care of the check?

A. Yes. As a rule, whoever extends the invitation is responsible for picking up the tab. And since your boss didn't take the initiative, it was up to you to take care of the check and then put it on your expense report so that you could get reimbursed.

Q. During a recent business luncheon I accidentally spilled some coffee. Some of the spill landed on the suit of the person who was seated next to me. Although I apologized profusely when it happened, I didn't realize until I returned to my office that I should have offered to pay to have the suit dry-cleaned. Is it still appropriate to extend that offer?

A. Definitely. I recommend you send the person a note with a check for the approximate cost of having the suit dry-cleaned.

Q. Is it ever appropriate to request a doggy bag following a meal?

A. If it is a business meal, it is not appropriate. If you are participating in a meal with friends or family, it's appropriate to have food boxed when half or more of your meal has not been eaten and/or the server makes the recommendation.

11.

The Etiquette of Tipping

The intent of tipping is universal—to ensure prompt service or to offer thanks for the delivery of prompt service.

Tipping has been around since the eighteenth century; and from all indications, it's here to stay. Whom to tip and when may not change either; but you can bet the "how much" element will continue to escalate.

So let's take a look at the proper way to handle this popular practice.

What the tip means
There are two kinds of tipping: the *influential* tip and the *thank-you* tip.

The influential tip is what you might give to a maitre d' who has reserved your favorite table for you. This kind of tip is generally given to a person to show your appreciation for a service that's been rendered or a favor that's been done for you.

The thank-you tip is a form of acknowledgment that you give to a person who has performed a service for you (served you, met your requests, etc.). This kind of tip should be given after the service has been rendered.

When? Where? How much?
Following are some guidelines to help you determine just how thankful you should be in various situations. Let's begin with restaurant personnel.

-–0 **Maitre d'.** If you're a regular patron of a restaurant, consider giving $10 or $20 to the maitre d' after every few visits.

-–0 **Captain.** This person should receive 25 percent of the tip you are leaving. For example, if you leave a 20-percent tip on a check totalling $100, $5 of your $20 tip should be given to the captain. You may deliver the tip to this person by specifying his portion of the gratuity on the bill. Or you may hand it to him when you leave.

☞ **Server.** The tip for this person should be 15- to 20-percent of the total check. (Be sure to base your tip on the pretax amount.) If you have received outstanding service, 20 percent should be rendered.

   ☞ Note: A tip of 15-percent of the pretax bill should also be left for servers at a buffet.

Busboy. The restaurant manager should deliver a portion of the 15- to 20-percent tip left for a server to this person.

☞ **Bartender.** Fifteen percent of your tab total (and no less than 50¢) should be left for the bartender.

☞ **Sommelier.** Leave a $3 to $5 tip to your wine steward for opening the bottle at your table and also for replenishing your glasses. You may give the tip directly to him or her, leave it with the maitre d', or specify the amount you are leaving for this person on your bill.

☞ **Coat-room attendant.** A good rule of thumb is to leave 50¢ per coat or item.

☞ **Parking valet.** One or two dollars should be given when your car is parked for you and returned to you.

☞ **Washroom attendant.** If you have accepted a towel or related service from this person, 50¢ to $1 is in order.

   Tipping is also in order for many hotel employees. Here's a guideline.

☞ **Shuttle driver.** When taking a courtesy shuttle from the airport to your hotel, it is definitely in order to tip the driver 15 percent of what it would have cost if you were driven by taxi.

← **Bellman.** This person should receive 50¢ to $1 per bag, both when you are shown to your room and upon departure.

← **Chambermaid.** If you are a hotel guest for three to five days, it is appropriate to leave a tip ($5, for example) for your room maid. Leave it on the dresser in an envelope marked, "Chambermaid," or leave the marked envelope with the desk clerk as you are checking out.

← **Room service.** It's most appropriate to add 15 percent to the check. Sometimes the gratuity is already added in—so be sure to read what you're signing.

← **Doorman.** When a taxi is hailed for you, the doorman should receive $1. Some doormen also expect to receive a tip even if a taxi is already available and they merely open and close the door for you. In such cases you'll have to just use your best judgment.

← **Housekeeping.** The delivery person who brings you a hair dryer or iron and ironing board should receive at least $1.

← **Concierge.** When a special service has been performed (such as procuring difficult-to-obtain theater tickets or airline reservations) a $5-to-$10 tip should be given upon completion of the service requested or prior to checking out.

← **Taxi driver.** It's customary to tip 15 percent of the fare.

Typical tipping blunders
With those guides in place, remember to steer clear of the common tipping blunders by adopting the following half-percents.

← Be prepared for tipping. Never wangle out of leaving a tip by making the excuse that you have only large bills with you.

← Plan ahead. Have your tip money available in hand or in pocket to avoid fumbling around for it.

← Leave a bill, rather than a pile of loose change, as a tip.

← When the position warrants it, always tip the person who has served you—even if it's likely you'll never encounter him or her again.

← Be discreet about tallying the amount of your tip. Never, for instance, use a calculator at the table for this purpose.

☛ Leave a small tip, even if the service was poor. If you were not pleased with the service, simply don't return.

Commonly Asked Questions About Tipping

Q. When I am on an expense account and want to leave an appropriate tip for a restaurant captain, sommelier, etc., how do you suggest this be handled?

A. Pay the bill by credit card and specify how you would like to have the tip divided.

Q. When is a gift appropriate as a tip?

A. Only during the holidays. If you choose to do this, the recipient should be someone with whom you deal regularly (answering-service operator, doorman, etc.). Also, be sure that you know the person's tastes.

Q. Recently I was entertaining out-of-town clients in a Mexican restaurant. A group of strolling musicians approached our table and serenaded us. Was a tip in order?

A. While tipping is always appreciated, in a situation such as you've described, it's not necessary if you have not made a specific request.

12.

Etiquette en Route

While we're all fairly good about extending etiquette to those who have a direct and continued impact on our lives, we sometimes fall short when it comes to travel etiquette. Maybe that's because many of the courtesies that are extended while traveling by air, car, or ship are typically observed as ritualistic in nature.

Still, as business professionals our goal should always be to maintain a polished image. This chapter presents some timely travel tips to help establish you as a seasoned and savvy traveler.

Flight manners
Because of the lightening-fast pace of our personal and professional lives these days, air travel has become commonplace. Unfortunately, we can't always say that about the good manners of those who jet from one destination to another.

Following are some suggestions for making your next air trip both comfortable and in keeping with your professional image.

"Excuse me. I need to get out."
🛬 Once you're seated, leaving your seat should be the exception rather than the rule. If you find that getting up and moving around is typically part of your travel ritual, then plan ahead and request an aisle seat.

Meetings in the air
If you're traveling with an associate, supervisor, or customer and plan to discuss business on the plane, arrange for your seats to be next to, rather than across the aisle from, one another. Not only will other airline passengers appreciate not having to overhear

your meeting, you will be more apt to maintain the confidentiality of your company business.

Respecting your fellow passenger

During flights, some people like to strike up a conversation with the person next to them; others do not. "En route" etiquette dictates that before trying to strike up a conversation, you tune into your fellow passenger's body language, to look for nonverbal clues as to whether the person seated next to you is interested in chatting. Needless to say, it's of utmost importance that you respect your fellow-passenger's wishes. Assuming you haven't observed any body language to indicate that your fellow passenger is opposed to conversing, it's appropriate to initiate a conversation either after your beverage has arrived or when the meal is first served. If your fellow passenger's response is brief and not followed by a question or commentary, take a hint.

Respecting flight attendants

It goes without saying that flight attendants should be treated with respect. If you have a question, for example, pose it when you are being served. Never ring the call bell for an attendant unless it's an emergency. In other words, extend the same courtesy to these professionals that you would to restaurant servers. If you'd like something, ask with a polite, "When you have a minute, may I have . . ." You can be assured they'll appreciate your respect for their time.

Flight farewells

Although a smile and a good-bye are commonplace as you are exiting a plane, few passengers (or flight-crew members, for that matter) incorporate a thank-you in their farewells. If you've never said "thank you" as you deboarded a plane, try it next time. You'll probably catch the crew off guard and even receive a comment of gratitude in return. No matter what distance you've traveled on a flight, a smile and a thank-you go a long way.

Air travel attire

If you're traveling during the work day, wear business attire. If you're traveling after 6 p.m., "business casual" is acceptable (a blazer and skirt for women; sport coat and trousers for men). Many business people find that on weekends the travel dress code can be even more casual (skorts or slacks and matching tops for women; polo shirt and slacks for men). No matter when you travel and what you choose to wear, however, be assured that the way you're dressed affects the way you're treated.

Traveling by car
Believe it or not, even everyday car travel has its own set of etiquette standards. As with much of the business of manners, most are based on courtesy and common sense.

When you're the driver. When you transport passengers, in many ways you're like a host or hostess who has invited guests into his or her domain. Enhance your role by observing the following amenities:

╼ Recognize that your car is an extension of your office. Rather than making excuses for your back seat or trunk being a mess, plan ahead. Be certain that your vehicle is clean inside and out. The way your car is maintained is a direct reflection on you.

╼ With the advent of electronic door locks, it has become rare for a driver to manually unlock the door for his passenger(s) when entering the vehicle. Whether you are a man or a woman, I recommend you still extend this courtesy to those who are "guests" in your car. Just think of it as akin to opening the door of your office or home and inviting someone in. Simply insert the key, unlock the car and open the door. Your passenger(s) can take it from there.

╼ Be tuned into the music preferences of your passenger(s). Often the best choice is to simply keep the radio off and use this time for conversation.

╼ Ask your passenger(s) whether they'd like the radio or the air conditioner higher or lower, etc.

When you're the passenger. When you're being driven to and from a destination, you are in essence, a guest in someone else's space. It follows, then, that your manners should reflect that status. Consider the following etiquette when you're in the passenger's seat.

╼ Let the person driving set the tone. Some drivers like to talk a lot; others, very little.

╼ Allow the driver to ask *you* whether you'd like the radio on, the air conditioner higher or lower, etc.

Careless car manners. It's easy to fall into etiquette traps when traveling by car with colleagues and other business associates. Avoid the three-most-common car faux pas by observing the following half-percents:

☛ Use your car for its intended purpose—not as a dressing room. In other words, women: Refrain from using the rear view mirror to check on your hairdo and makeup. And for goodness' sake, avoid putting on lipstick en route. This seemingly insignificant little gesture has a terrible effect on your professional image.

☛ If you must eat en route, be discreet. Never, for instance, pop in french fries two at a time. Observe the same high standards of etiquette reserved for the table—as much as possible under the circumstances, of course.

☛ Fill up your gas tank before picking up your passenger(s). If you're on an extended trip, of course, it becomes necessary to stop and "fill 'er up." Whenever possible, however, avoid this practice.

Taxi tidbits

Unless you're in Australia (remember where Crocodile Dundee sat when he traveled by cab through New York City?), it's most appropriate to sit in the back seat. If, however, more than two people are traveling in the same cab, it's perfectly acceptable for the senior associate(s) to be offered the back seat by the junior associate(s), one of whom may take the front seat.

One of those awkward moments of hesitation often arises when it comes time to pay the taxi tab—particularly when the passengers occupy different levels in the business pecking order. I always recommend that junior executives be prepared to take care of the fare if their senior counterparts do not make the initiative to do so. This, again, is one of those play-it-by-ear situations.

Commonly Asked Questions About Etiquette en Route

Q. Once in a while I fly first class. In several instances I've made the following observation. Some flight attendants address male passengers by "Mr." and their last names, making no attempt to address women who are flying first class with the same courtesy. What do you think about this?

A. It's certainly a nice touch to address people by name.

When extending the courtesy of addressing people by name, flight attendants should be consistent, addressing their male and female passengers in the same manner.

Q. Last week I returned from an out-of-town business trip with my boss. This was my first company trip, and I experienced several awkward moments. I wasn't sure, for instance, whether I should offer to take care of tips, hail taxis, make dinner reservations, etc. As a result, I waited for my boss to take the lead. What should I have done?

A. When executives of unequal rank travel together, the junior person should handle trip details—tipping, hailing taxis, etc. When it comes to checking in and out of hotels, each party is responsible for making the necessary arrangements.

Since this was your first business trip, it sounds as if you've gotten off to a good start. It was wise of you to let your boss take the lead and observe his or her actions.

13.

International Etiquette

Believe it or not . . . in our jet-set, small-world, global society, there *is* a universal language. It's called the smile.

This basic gesture, a gift bestowed on human beings and on no other living species, is truly the golden rule for international communications.

Unfortunately, things get more complex from that point on.

As you've no doubt noticed, this is the shortest chapter in the book. That's because a thorough, practical treatment of international etiquette warrants a book in itself.

If you're curious about this subject or if you know that your business plans call for a trip abroad in the coming weeks, months, or years, take a look at the list of suggested readings included at the end of this book. A number of professionals whose expertise I respect have addressed international etiquette in a thorough and interesting manner.

Since most of us have already encountered or will work closely with people from other countries and cultures, I do recommend a few basic guidelines.

Recognize cultural differences
Aside from the smile, the first rule of communicating with international colleagues is to recognize that people from other countries have markedly different lifestyles and often work under business systems different from ours.

If you're unfamiliar with some of these customs and manners, your best approach is the one I have already recommended for those moments of hesitation. Simply take your cue from those around you. In this way you should be able to establish a comfort level for associating with visitors and immigrants to our country, as well as the people of the countries to which you travel.

Handshakes

Cultures can often be miles apart in more ways than mere geographic distance. Simple issues like space can cause many awkward moments. In some cultures, for example, it is offensive to stand too close to someone. In others the issue of touch is a sensitive one. This is one reason the question of handshakes consistently comes up in the international communications section of our business etiquette seminars. Women, especially, often ask whether it's appropriate to extend their hand to colleagues in foreign lands.

The answer depends on the customs and mores of the country. In Europe, for instance, the handshake is quite common and is used as the customary greeting with people who are meeting for the first time. It's also a gesture commonly exchanged by coworkers. Note: It's still in order for women to initiate handshakes with men in European countries.

In the Middle East, however, it's a different story. Once upon a time Middle Eastern tradition discouraged women from touching the hand of an Arab until he initiated the handshake. Since many of these customs are in the midst of transition, that may have changed. Again, a glance at one of the excellent books dealing with this subject will answer your specific questions.

Communication caveats

To set the tone when communicating with business people from various backgrounds and cultures, begin with a few basic points. These guidelines are from Norm Oches, Vice President for Global Marketing and World Travel at G-Force in Charlotte North Carolina.

➡ Start slowly. Remember, your international colleagues not only have to absorb what you're saying, they also have to become used to how you sound. That includes voice quality, accent, speed of delivery, etc. For instance, if a person does not respond correctly to a question, it does not necessarily mean that he or she didn't know the answer. Rather, he or she may not have understood the question.

➡ When convenient and appropriate, use a pointer. In meetings and workshops involving overheads, board work, charts, etc., use of this tool will help your international audience focus on the concepts under discussion.

➡ Use jokes sparingly. Be cautious about using jokes or other forms of humor to loosen up your audience. Telling a successful joke during a business presentation is an art. Attempting a joke in an international setting can be downright risky because of cultural differences.

⊷ Follow the KISS rule. Keep it simple, stupid! Gear the level of your presentation to the largest number of people possible. Use as many charts and diagrams as you can to illustrate the concepts in your presentation.

Finally, a caution statement from At Ease. For all the importance of simplicity and practical teaching techniques when working with international colleagues, as business professionals we must be sensitive to our visitors' reactions and careful not to appear condescending in anything we do or say. Respecting the expertise, professionalism, and cultures of our visitors *without* appearing to talk down to them is a fine line to tread. And that brings us back to the starting point of this chapter.

If you want to get a lot of mileage from your associations with international colleagues, learn to speak the universal language: the smile. For interpersonal communication that simple gesture can go a long way—even around the world!

14.

Manners for Special Occasions

So far we've discussed manners and etiquette as they relate to the everyday situations and events of today's business environment. But what about those special occasions often observed on the work scene? Holidays, weddings, births—how do these fit in with a professional, polished image? Let's talk about them.

Holiday etiquette

The weeks between Thanksgiving and the holidays annually bring on a slate of special activities and events. In some companies personnel bring in cookies or holiday punch to share with their coworkers. Many exchange greetings and cards. Companies, too, often send "official" holiday greeting cards to their clients, suppliers, and colleagues.

In addition, most offices plan some sort of in-house celebration just before the traditional holiday break. Many employees even find themselves invited to holiday open houses in the homes of supervisors and coworkers. All this can be very enjoyable. Just remember: An ambiance of merriment and celebration in the business environment doesn't mean we can let down our guard on appropriate behavior and etiquette. Following, then, is a list of do's and don'ts to guide you through the annual holiday season.

Holiday greeting cards

━━◐ It's become traditional for companies to order imprinted holiday greetings. While these cards are usually quite attractive, you can add a feeling of warmth by personalizing them with a short, handwritten greeting. We're not talking about an epistle here. Just a short note, like, "Thank you for your interest in working together." Or, "Looking forward to seeing you after the first of the year."

As emphasized throughout this book, those extra little touches often reap the largest rewards.

Observing the social graces

In the hustle and bustle of the holiday season, it's easy to lose sight of the fact that when you're invited to a social event on your employer's or customer's turf, it's a social occasion, certainly—but one with political overtones.

For some reason, people often view business/social occasions in a different light during the holidays. Maybe it's the spirit of the season. Spirit or no spirit, however, the basic social graces still apply.

So remember some of the points discussed in chapter 9, The Art of Mingling. At informal receptions such as holiday cocktail parties and open houses, don't mix only with those whose company you enjoy most. Mingle and make small talk with those you don't know well or at all. It's a gesture that will be noticed and appreciated by your host.

Playing cook and maid

When you're the host or hostess for a holiday gathering of business associates, you should be just that—and not the cook and maid, too.

By demonstrating your role as a gracious host or hostess, you may be priming yourself for that next promotion—or that of your spouse. So rather than running back and forth to the kitchen to replenish the hors d'oeuvres tray, greet and meet people, introduce them to one another, make small talk—and above all, enjoy yourself!

Ignoring spouses

Holiday gatherings are often the only time during the year that spouses are invited to business/social events. In my business etiquette columns and workshops, I frequently hear from spouses (generally women) about their unpleasant experiences. Here's an excerpt from a typical letter.

"I lose my identity at these parties. Rather than being Mary Smith, John Smith's spouse, I'm John's wife, Mary. The typical questions I'm asked are, 'How are the kids?' or, 'Have you finished your holiday shopping?' I would rather be asked about my job and interests.

"And I'm not a leper," this woman eloquently emphasizes. "My husband is greeted with a handshake; and what do I get? A nod, if I'm lucky, or a pat on the shoulder."

Unfortunately, there are still people who need to be reminded about this kind of behavior. If you're one of them, it's time you got with the program!

Happy Holidays! vs. Merry Christmas!

━━0 Whether you're answering the company phone or speaking to clients face to face, choose your holiday greeting according to the recipient. Your Jewish associates, for instance, will respect and welcome your Happy Hanukkah wishes. If you're not aware of the religious affiliations of the persons you're greeting, play it safe and offer generic but nonetheless sincere Happy Holidays!

Gift-giving customs

━━0 If you decide to send your Chinese client a gift, be sure it's not a clock. Why? It's a symbol of bad luck in their culture. And in the Japanese tradition, the manner in which the gift is wrapped is just as important as the gift itself. As a successful business person in today's global society, you need to be tuned in to such subtleties. The same holds true here at home and in your work place.

━━0 Become aware of the particular gift-giving customs (or lack thereof) in your own business environment. Is it cricket, for instance, to reward your staff with a holiday gift? That's something you'll have to determine. Often a supervisor will treat his or her staff to a holiday lunch.

Is it appropriate to say Happy Holidays to your supervisor with a gift? Again, what's the tradition in your work place? To avoid appearing flashy with expensive presents, employees will often bring in homemade cookies, fudge, punch, or some other treat (even "store-bought" goodies) to be shared. In most business environments, this is viewed as a friendly and enjoyable display of holiday spirit. Again, your particular business culture will determine what's most appropriate.

Office birthday parties

As with other events, office birthday parties should be celebrated according to company policy and precedent. Some organizations celebrate birthdays by announcing them in their internal publication or during monthly meetings. Other firms have a birthday card sent by the president. Still others may arrange to have a cake or gift, if the birthday is a significant one.

If a company policy has not yet been set, it should be recognized that once something has been done, it sets a precedent for how people will expect such occasions to be handled in the future. The key to celebrating office birthdays is consistency.

Commonly Asked Questions About Manners for Special Occasions

Q. I am a department manager and will soon be getting married. My fiance and I have limited our guest list. My questions are these: If I invite my four managers and my boss, is it necessary for me also to invite the three staff people who report directly to me? Since the wedding is on a Saturday afternoon and evening, am I also required to invite their spouses?

A. My answer is "yes" to both questions. If you will be inviting your managers, it's also in your best interests, politically, to invite those with whom you work closely. And yes, spouses must be included.

15.

Men and Women as Colleagues

The last few decades have brought about numerous changes in the business world. In addition to advances in technology, we have watched the advance of women to top professional levels in the corporate arena and as business owners. This climb has created transitions and confusion in the codes of etiquette. While men are often left scratching their heads about acceptable social amenities, women find themselves needing to master levels of awareness about things their mothers may never have taught them.

Because most of the etiquette tips addressed to this late-twentieth-century phenomenon have been covered in a general way elsewhere in this book, this chapter is intended as a review, to give added emphasis to the special problems raised by issues of gender.

Greetings and introductions

Many men were reared to believe it was improper to initiate a handshake with a woman. When the role of women was strictly "raising the family" and perhaps belonging to a garden club, the initiation of a handshake by a man was perceived as overly aggressive. Times change, but habits die hard. Today, if a man is meeting three men and a woman, it's natural for him to extend his hand to the men, saying, "It's nice to meet you. It's nice to meet you. It's nice to meet you." When it comes to the woman, however, what does he do? While some men initiate a handshake to the woman, others might substitute a mere nod. Why? Because many of these men were raised believing they should wait for a woman to offer her hand. They're doing what their mothers taught them.

Because some men are still ginchy on this point of etiquette, women sometimes have to give men a hand (literally) and initiate the handshake. But men, if a woman doesn't take the initiative, for heaven's sake get that hand out there. I guarantee you will offend most of today's women more by *not* offering your hand.

It's stand-up time

When a man and woman are dining together in a business situation, the woman generally appreciates having the man stand to acknowledge her departure and return. If the business woman with whom you're dining is uncomfortable with your extending this social amenity, she'll let you know by saying something like, "That's not necessary."

On-the-street manners

Whether you're in a business or a social setting, "walking" rules still apply on the street.

While it's no longer necessary, it's still appreciated when a man walks on the outside, closest to the curb. This is one of those social amenities women still enjoy—not because we're afraid of getting splashed. We simply appreciate the courtesy.

Hand-in-glove etiquette

Here's another stumper. It's winter and you're walking down the street wearing an overcoat and gloves. You meet someone you know. Should you remove your right glove before shaking hands? Unless it's bitter cold, my recommendation is, certainly!

Women hosts

Many women today find themselves inviting male colleagues to lunch. What's the most diplomatic way to let the server know you'll be taking care of the check?

As a woman, you will be asked to order first. When the server requests your order, simply say, "I'd like my guest to go first." You'll be accomplishing two things with this response. You'll let the server know who should receive the check, and you'll be putting your guest at ease by confirming that this lunch is on you.

Applying lipstick at the table

This issue is one of the most hotly debated points in today's new etiquette codes. Is it acceptable for women to apply lipstick at the table during a business luncheon? At workshops, to determine a pragmatic answer to this question, I always ask for a show of hands (from both men and women) regarding their preferences. Two suggestions invariably win hands down. Either go without lipstick, say the majority, or excuse yourself to apply it. The reaction to reapplying lipstick at the table puts this gesture right down there with a man combing his hair or using a toothpick at the table.

Who's on first?

When it comes to introductions, this question needn't be as confusing as the classic Abbott and Costello routine.

To determine whose name to say first when introducing a man and a woman to each other in a business setting, base your decision on your relationship with the people involved. For example, if the man is your customer and the woman is your supervisor, the man's name should be said first.

Elevators and other curious contraptions

Elevators. Is there a pecking order to exiting an elevator?

The answer to, "Who should leave the elevator first—man or woman?" is quite simple: the person closest to the door should exit first. If a man and a woman are at an equal distance from the door, of course a man should motion for a woman to exit first. If, however, a man is closest to the door and has one or more women behind him, it's acceptable for him to exit first and simply hold the door for the women as they exit.

Escalators. When a man and woman are ascending an escalator, who should get on first? If you said a man should allow a woman to precede him, you're right.

When descending an escalator, it's most appropriate for a man to precede a woman, turning around to face her as soon as he gets on.

Revolving doors. Here's another "who comes first?" Who should go through a revolving door first? Believe it or not, a man should precede a woman. As he's going through, it's appropriate for him to say something like, "Let me get the door for you."

Whatever you do, don't get in together!

Faux pas made by men
Many men are still uncertain about some of the fine points of male/female working relationships. Here are a few of the most serious business etiquette faux pas committed by men.

- ◆ Addressing female colleagues as "honey," "dear" or "sweetheart."

- ◆ Touching or patting female colleagues rather than greeting them with a handshake.

- ◆ Excluding women from the "Old Boys' Network."

Faux pas made by women
Even with these indiscretions, men are still ahead of the game in many ways. Men have the past on which to base some of their present actions; women don't. Most of our mothers and grandmothers raised families rather than working outside the home. Of those who did have jobs outside the home, very few were in management. Our background may help explain these common faux pas.

- ◆ Giving only our first names when answering the phone. When only a first name is used, business women are frequently mistaken as employees who have responsibility without authority.

- ◆ Giggling to fill pauses.

- ◆ Not being as friendly with the spouses of male associates as we are with the associates. More than anything, this is probably a sensitivity issue. When attending a business or social function to which spouses and "significant others" are invited, you should go out of your way to be as cordial to your associate's or customer's spouse as you are to the associate. Your friendliness and genuine interest in the person will go a long way.

- ◆ Using foul language in the work place. Profanity has no place anywhere—particularly in the work place. Using profanity is perceived as lacking vocabulary.

- ◆ Making personal telephone calls on the job. With women juggling nine-to-five jobs and family responsibilities, it's understandable that personal calls need to be made on the job from time to time. They should, however, be the exception rather than the rule. And when possible, they should be made on break time or during the lunch hour. By the way, it's also perceived as unprofessional to habitually receive personal calls.

Commonly Asked Questions About Men and Women as Colleagues

Q. As I was returning to work after lunch yesterday, I saw one of my business associates walking on the other side of the street. He was with a woman who appeared to be his girlfriend. I was going to wave hello to my colleague, but he appeared to be engrossed in conversation and was rather blatant in his display of physical contact with this person. His actions did not match his personal attire. Please discuss the importance of public manners in the work place.

A. Displays of affection should be reserved for appropriate environments—generally far removed from the work place.

Q. When speaking to a group of business women, is it appropriate to refer to them as *ladies, females,* or *women*?

A. When business women were asked this question, the overwhelming majority said they prefer *"women."*

Q. Our staff consists of four women and one man. Each of us is responsible for cleaning up different areas of the office. The man, however, seems to have the mistaken impression that we will clean up after him. One disturbing problem, in particular, is that he leaves the toilet seat up. We have confronted him about this matter, but it has done no good. Not only is his action an annoyance to us, we're concerned about our customers, who are primarily women and who have access to the bathroom.

A. If the man you're describing happens to be your supervisor, I recommend that you not bring up the subject again. If, however, he is a coworker and reports to one of the women concerned, perhaps she could discuss this matter with him in private. As a last resort, you could post a letter in the bathroom stating, "We, the women in the office, are down when you continue to leave the seat up." Sometimes a little humor can be effective—even for a problem like this, which is a perennial complaint of women but never seems to bother men.

Q. When men inquire about family members, I frequently hear them ask, "How's the wife?" Please let these men know that "the" describes objects. The phrase should be replaced by "your wife."

A. You're right on target there! My guess is that this term is used out of habit more than anything else. Perhaps your letter will raise the level of awareness of men who unknowingly make this mistake.

Q. I recently found myself in an awkward situation as the only woman in an all-male managerial group meeting. Before our monthly meeting got started, someone asked if we could arrange to get coffee. Many eyes turned in my direction. I read this gesture as a cue that they expected me to jump up and get it.

Rather than let these male chauvinists appoint me as their gofer, I said, "Coffee sounds good to me, too. I'll have mine black."

When they realized I wasn't going to get the coffee, one of the other managers stepped outside the meeting room and asked a member of our support staff to arrange for coffee.

Had I been in a room with only women, I would have initiated the request for coffee in a minute. In the situation I was in, however, I felt the way I handled it was most appropriate. What do you think?

A. Congratulations! It sounds as if your action (or lack of) set the tone for future meetings.

Q. What's the best way to react to dirty jokes? I've been in uncomfortable situations when men I hardly know tell off-color jokes that I find offensive in a business environment. If I ignore them, I feel as though I'm considered a prude; if I respond by laughing, I feel as though I'm lowering myself to the joke-teller's level. How should a woman react in a situation like this?

A. The person who is telling an off-color joke in a business setting should be sensitive to the taste of others. If there's even the slightest chance that someone might be offended, it would be preferable not to tell the joke.

As to how you should react, after the joke has been told and reactions to it have ceased, simply change the tone of the conversation by asking a work-related question.

Q. Several years ago I acquired a habit of winking. For me, winking serves as a way of acknowledging someone I know but am too far away from to talk with. I also use this nonverbal gesture instead of smiling or as reinforcement that someone did a good job.

As harmless as I perceive this gesture to be, one of the women in my department mentioned that she found my winking to be a distracting habit. She also said that some women may perceive it as demeaning. What do you think?

A. Although your winking may be harmless, it serves no purpose in the work place. Winking is generally perceived as a flirtatious gesture. Perhaps it would be better simply to smile.

Q. Is it appropriate for a woman to say something to a man whose zipper is unzipped?

A. My recommendation is that you mention your observation to one of your other male associates, who can then bring it to the man's attention. By doing so, you spare the person the embarrassment of hearing it from a woman.

Epilogue

You were probably already a polished individual before you picked up this book—otherwise you would most likely never have been intrigued by the title in the first place. None of us is perfect, however. I hope you've picked up some additional suggestions and advice for helping you move more quickly along the road to business success.

Believe it or not . . . even after five years of dealing with business etiquette on a daily basis, I'm still learning. And the enjoyable aspect of my education is that I'm learning from people like you— the ones who attend my seminars and who phone our Business Etiquette Hotline with questions and comments.

Because you've read my book, I consider you a client of sorts. So if you have other business etiquette questions, please call our Hotline: 800-873-9909 (8:30 am–5:00 pm EST). I hope I'm available to speak with you personally. If not, one of our competent staff members will be happy to take your call.

And because excellent communication and networking are so enjoyable and so important, both in our personal and professional lives, please do me a favor and share this book with a friend or colleague. Maybe we can even call that gesture a half-percent, don't you think?

List of Recommended Readings

Axtell, Roger. *Do's and Taboos Around the World*. Compiled by The Parker Pen Company. 2nd edition. New York: John Wiley & Sons, Inc., 1990.

Axtell, Roger. *Do's and Taboos of Hosting International Visitors*. New York: John Wiley & Sons, Inc., 1990.

Axtell, Roger. *Gestures*. New York: John Wiley & Sons, Inc., 1991.

Letitia Baldridge's Complete Guide to Executive Manners. Edited by Sandi Gelles-Cole. New York: Rawson Associates, 1985.

Letitia Baldridge's Complete Guide to the New Manners for the '90s. New York: Rawson Associates, 1990.

Bixler, Susan. *The Professional Image*. New York: Perigree Books, Putnam, 1984.

Brooks, Michael. *Instant Rapport*. New York: Warner Books, 1989.

Doyle, Michael with David Straus. *How to Make Meetings Work*. New York: Jove Books, 1976.

Jankowic, Elena, with Sandra Bernstein. *Behave Yourself!* Englewood Cliffs, N.J.: Prentice-Hall, 1986.

Martin, Phyllis. *Word Watchers Handbook*. 3rd edition. New York: St. Martin's Press, 1991.

Martin, Phyllis. *Martin's Magic Formula For Getting The Right Job*. 2nd edition. New York: St. Martin's Press, 1987.

Phillips, Linda and Wayne, with Lynne Rogers. *The Concise Guide to Executive Etiquette*. Garden City, N.Y.: Doubleday, 1990.

Pincus, Marilyn. *Mastering Business Etiquette and Protocol*. New York: National Institute of Business Management, Inc., 1988.

Rowland, Diana. *Japanese Business Etiquette*. New York: Warner Books, 1985.

Sell, Shawn. "Office Party Etiquette: Holiday Dress for Business Success." *USA Today*, November 30, 1988, p. 4D.

Stewart, Marjabelle Young. *The New Etiquette*. New York: St. Martin's Press, 1987.

Wyse, Lois. *Company Manners*. New York: McGraw-Hill, 1987.

Index